CW00553594

Websites
For Business
Managers

i

Websites for Business Managers

How to Confidently Work with IT Staff, Decode Geek-Speak, and Create the Website Your Business Needs

Website Wisdom Collection

Chris Davidson

Cover by Scott Graham

Typesetting by Megan Sheer

Websites for Business Managers by Chris Davidson

ISBN (1st Edition)   978-1-7392307-4-6

Embarkation Check

You are about to embark on a journey, and I want to make sure you have the best possible travel guide, based on what you do and the questions you're likely to ask.

The multifaceted nature of websites can make them complex to understand. Your business role alters how you view your organization's website, and therefore, what you ought to know. This is true for many endeavours. For example, you'd expect *The Photographers Guide to Portrait Photography* to cover both equipment and concepts. You'd expect chapters on lenses, focus, framing, depth of field, etc. You'd also welcome content addressing the set; indoor versus outdoor, group versus solo shoots, etc. You might also find material about posing models: lighting, makeup, clothing, etc. Now suppose the same author publishes *The Model's Guide to Portrait Photography*—how will it differ from the first book? There will be some overlap in content, but with different emphasis and detail levels. You'd expect symmetry and compatibility between the two books, as opposed to radically different or opposing content.

So too with *Websites for Business Managers* and *Why Your Website Doesn't Work*, published earlier in 2023. Both books address the same subject, but from the perspectives of different readers.

I wrote *Websites for Business Managers* for:

- People in a business leadership position (e.g. team leader, department head, divisional director, company board director).

- People who aren't website specialists and sometimes feel out of their depth in discussions with IT professionals.

- People who see the company website as more central to the work their department does.

- People working in a business that's big enough to need an IT department (even if it uses a high percentage of contract staff).

If you're one of these business leaders, then reading *Websites for Business Managers* will give you:

- The confidence to engage with IT professionals and represent what (your part of) the business needs from the website.

- Simple explanations of important website-related terminology, so you don't get bamboozled by geek-speak.

- An understanding of what other companies are doing with their websites, so you can benchmark your own approach.

In *Websites for Business Managers*, I've aligned the content with job positions familiar to non-IT managers. This is to remove any mystique surrounding the technicalities of 'websites' and instead, treat them as if they were simply 'another employee'.

What about the earlier book, *Why Your Website Doesn't Work*? Who's it for and what does it give readers that's different?

Why Your Website Doesn't Work is for:

- Solopreneurs—people who do everything themselves, including briefing contracted help, such as website designers.

- Owners of small, service-oriented businesses, who 'own' the website because their company is too small to have full-time support staff.

- Entrepreneurs who have a business idea, but no website, and need help to develop their website and online presence.

Why Your Website Doesn't Work takes a detailed approach to websites and their alignment with what you sell and to whom. You'll find an online assessment that reports your website's effectiveness against five criteria and suggests what you should fix first. Readers can also download a software tool to help in creating highly effective product descriptions—the software guide is included as part of the book.

Why Your Website Doesn't Work delivers a thorough analysis for people who want to get to grips with their website's inefficiencies. They want to do this before asking others for help, as they've previously ended up spending a ton of money with the wrong people, on the wrong things.

In summary, *Websites for Business Managers*—the book you're reading right now—gives business leaders a head start in two important areas; (i) a better understanding of how websites can improve businesses, and (ii) greater confidence to contribute to website projects and engage IT professionals in website-related conversations.

You'll find more about other books in the *Website Wisdom Collection* at the back of this book.

Contents

LAZY WEBSITES FIXED IN FIVE

Why You, Why Now?

The COVID-19 pandemic opened the third decade of this century with a bang and the echoes will reverberate for many years to come. Economies and communities have changed forever. Your working life will never return to its pre-COVID state (even if you, or your employer can remember what that was). This is a business book, so, with no offence intended, I put aside the terrible personal tragedies the pandemic wrought and focus on the permanent changes it imposed on the way you and I work.

For example, as part of the first COVID-19 national lockdown, the UK government suspended all building work and closed the construction sector. The situation was grim: building sites lay empty and silent, as did all the companies making up the vast supply chain of the construction sector.

One smart building-materials supplier could see the way the wind was blowing[1] To keep his business afloat, the owner laid off most of his staff, taking advantage of the government-backed staff-furlough scheme. He had previously invested in a capable website and believed strongly that technology was a driving force in his business. While the website's ecommerce capabilities weren't particularly well developed, the business had a good online stock database, including inventory levels, product descriptions, etc. Long-term investment in search engine optimization had resulted in the website getting lots of traffic and being well positioned in search engine returns.

---

1   A true story. The company is known to me but doesn't want to be named.

1

Confident in his vision, the owner poured a shedload of money into the website, most of which was spent on improving the ecommerce capabilities. Remember, this was when his business was producing zero income, and nobody knew when the economy would reopen.

When construction work restarted, this building supplies company ran rings around its competitors. The company was soon generating 80% of its pre-COVID revenue with 20% of the staff. Nowadays, the shop at the front of the yard is like a morgue. Tradespeople don't bother visiting anymore; they order online, directly from building sites, using their mobile phones. The business—and the sector it serves—profoundly reshaped itself.

It's true that this business owner was smart enough to see the change coming and reposition his business to capitalize on the opportunity. However, it was his steady investment in technology over the years that gave him the edge over his competitors. His website had firm foundations and was already performing well, making it easier to add additional capability.

From a business and technology perspective, I believe much of what happened during the pandemic would have happened at some point during this decade. A lot got squashed into a couple of years. There were some winners and many losers.

How about you? Where do you fit into all this? Whether you like it or not, you're in the mix somewhere, and knowing where will help you progress. I'm going to help you find out.

In my experience, the owner of the building supplies company was an exception. I've come across many people—business owners and employees—who have had a tough time. Talking of my experience, you deserve to know why you can trust me. I've been in IT for more than forty years—before the term 'information technology' even existed. I was part-author of the IBM Consulting Group methodology and later established the consulting services division for a specialist IT supplier within the aviation sector. I set up my consulting company over twenty years ago and have helped hundreds of clients improve their businesses. Since 2017, my colleagues and I have conducted an annual worldwide survey of thousands of business websites. I've presented the results at industry conferences on both sides of the Atlantic and Pacific. I know the challenges and I've created a successful team that helps clients overcome them.

Although many people view websites as being easy to create, implementing an effective, highly engaging business website is a different matter. Having one will make your employer's business more successful and knowing about them will make you more successful too. You need to know enough about websites to understand how your organization uses them, and—crucially for your career progression—how to lead the expansion of web-based services for your area of expertise.

I understand you may not be interested in websites for their own sake—you want to know more about how they can help you do your job better. Reading this book will achieve that.

You'll find chapters that explain some important IT lingo and help you make sense of it all. To be clear: this is not a book about information technology, nor am I attempting to convert you into a website expert. The world has all the website experts it needs. What it doesn't have is enough people like you: *people who know how to put websites to work, so that businesses can progress.*

So, why you? Because you're responsible for leading a team that has to change its way of working. Your colleagues will copy your lead. Your example and actions count.

And why now? Because a step change in working practices has just occurred and not everyone has noticed. You have—that's why you're here, reading this now.

Seize the day. Turn the page and crack on.

Part A

Quick Start Essentials

1.

Checklists for IT Projects

As websites spread their tentacles deeper within organizations, it's inevitable that people in leadership positions will become more involved in website projects. To get you off to a quick start, here's an overview of the important parts of a website development project (in approximate chronological order).

Each of the following topics could justify more detail and I revisit some later. Use the subheadings below as a quick checklist for website projects—to balance IT department input and ensure the business is being heard. Use this chapter to check the project is on track and covering everything it should.

This chapter will help you structure your interactions with your IT department colleagues. If you suspect something isn't being addressed, I'd urge you to call it out. I've seen too many projects go off the rails due to issues not being called out early on. The IT professionals will regard you as their 'business expert'. They want your help, so don't be shy or feel awkward because they've invited you to play in their backyard.

Website Project Audit Checklist

Website Purpose

Before anything else, make sure there's an agreed upon, clear understanding as to the website's purpose. There are three major categories of websites: ecommerce, information dissemination, and lead generation. To which does yours belong? For example, the BBC and CNN are information dissemination sites. Amazon is an ecommerce site. Most general business websites *should* contribute to the marketing efforts of the organization they represent. The fact that many don't can be put down to an initial lack of clarity.

A website's purpose impacts the design, functionality, and content. Clearly, the website must serve the business, so make sure the project team hears your voice.

Target Audience

Identify your target audience—the tighter the definition, the better. This helps tailor design, content, and functionality. The audience belongs to the business—not the IT department—so make sure your colleagues in IT hear your voice.

Website Builder Software

This falls within the remit of the IT department. However, you ought to take an interest in how the site's content will be managed. Who loads new content and maintains existing pages? If these tasks fall to a business department, then you'll want a tool that's easy for your colleagues to learn. They won't be using it every day, so a tool that needs a power-user for even simple updates will end up adding too much friction to website updates. Does the proposed software have good online support? Is training easily available?

Sitemap Creation

You can expect your IT colleagues to take the lead on this, but you should maintain an interest. A sitemap is a schematic list of all the pages on your website. Creating one helps organize the content and assign it to the correct pages. Act as the user's voice and tell the team how website users will (most likely) interact with the site and its content. Ensure the final sitemap makes sense to you. It's true that websites are very flexible and easy to change, but that 'easiness' is relative. All changes consume time and money: the fewer the better. Make changes when you're dealing with paper and pencil, rather than keyboards and code.

Design Selection

This is another area where you'd expect your IT colleagues to take the lead. However, I'd expect them to get marketing and brand management input from whoever owns those functions.

Content Development

A hugely important area and one that clearly belongs to the business and not your colleagues in IT. Content should be relevant to your target audience and align with your website's purpose. More on content later, but for the purpose of this checklist, make sure it's owned by a business department and well looked after. Good content is the most important contribution business departments make to website projects.

Testing

This is a pet peeve of mine and I revisit it later (see Chapter 9). For this high-level checklist (a) check that your IT colleagues have committed to a formal test plan and (b) ask what role they envisage for the business. In summary, the IT department should test the functionality and performance of the website, while the business should approve the content and how the site behaves for visitors. The business should formally 'accept' the site on behalf of the business (as part of the Customer Acceptance Test).

Launch

The launch of the new website is an important milestone. No matter how many times the new site has been checked during development, it's always worth verifying the content, buttons, forms, and links once the site is live to the world.

Monitoring

There are two parts to performance monitoring. Your colleagues in IT should look after the technicalities associated with the site being online, security, load speed, etc. Your contribution is to validate the usefulness of the content. Is it being read by the right audience? Are the lead magnets getting as many downloads as you envisaged? Are visitors getting lost in the navigation?

The Top 10 Mistakes in Website Projects

Any of the following should ring alarm bells. I've listed them in an approximate chronological order, i.e. the earlier items should be addressed at the planning stage (and are therefore furthest away from launch date).

1. Not having a clear strategy or purpose:

Without a clear purpose, it's difficult to create a website that meets the needs of the business and its customers. In my experience, this area is too frequently glossed over, in favour of having a website to 'keep up with the Joneses'.

2. Neglecting website optimization for search engines:

Search engine optimization (SEO) is important for long-term viability and traffic creation. It's a long and constant battle and consequently, is frequently side-lined. Keep at it.

3. Failing to prioritize user experience:

A website that is difficult to navigate is a big turn-off. Visitors will simply click away. Ensure the user experience is prioritized and the subsequent sites are easy to navigate.

4. Not optimizing for mobile devices:

More and more people are accessing the internet on mobile devices, so it's important for businesses to optimize their websites for mobile devices. As a case in point, I have a client whose website's mobile traffic is over 75% of the total. Expect this sort of profile if you deliver any form of personal service, for example, lawyer, psychologist, therapist.

5. Focusing too much on aesthetics:

Functionality is what counts. While having an attractive website is important, businesses shouldn't focus solely on aesthetics at the expense of functionality. I frequently find business departments getting excited by super-duper, whizzy, carousel thingamajigs, instead of focusing on what really counts—solving the visitor's problems.

6. Ignoring website security:

Please don't. This belongs to your colleagues in IT. All you can do is lean on them politely and swiftly respond to any threats they identify, or security actions they want you to take. Of course, you have ensured all your team members use strong passwords (and don't leave them on sticky notes next to their keyboards).

7. Not having clear calls-to-action:

Calls-to-action (CTAs) are important for guiding users toward desired actions, such as making a purchase or filling out a form. Double check CTAs are clear and easy to interpret.

8. Failing to create high-quality content:

High-quality content is important for engaging users and improving search engine rankings (see point 2 above). Business departments have a lot to contribute here—either creating the content or verifying material that's written by others. Don't let this responsibility slide, you're letting down the entire organization.

9. Neglecting website maintenance:

Although one for your IT colleagues, it deserves mention. If they ask for your help in testing a new fix, respond as promptly as you reasonably can—your fix may be one of many that need to be tested and applied according to a complex matrix of updates.

10. Not tracking website analytics:

Don't imagine that this is solely the responsibility of the IT department. Their job is to deliver a high performance website. You should take a strong interest in how visitors interact with its content—content you most likely took the lead in creating. Own your job, regardless of the platform.

Part A is all about giving you the confidence to engage with your technically minded colleagues and quiz them on the whys and wherefores of their suggestions. As useful as these checklists are, there remains an unavoidable minimum website vocabulary you ought to know. The next chapter uses a case study to introduce this and keep it firmly grounded within a business environment.

2.

Case Study Exemplar HR Portal

Companies create websites for different categories of users; *internal* and *external* being two major audiences. Although their needs are very different, the underpinning technicalities used to service the needs of both are frequently similar.

A detailed examination of Caterpillar Inc's website[2] reveals it to be as large as the company it represents. The company has done an excellent job and the site has clearly benefited from its owner's deep pockets. That said, companies with more modest budgets can learn a lot from studying Caterpillar's approach.

To be clear: I have no commercial relationship with Caterpillar, nor any inside knowledge. I'm viewing their website from a visitor's perspective, just like you.

Caterpillar's Exceptional HR Portal

While Caterpillar's website could serve as an exemplar for many aspects of website design, I want to focus on its excellent human resources portal. This aspect of their site makes a magnificent case study because it illustrates:

• A neat solution to a problem facing many organizations—that of attracting and managing top-class talent.

2   https://www.caterpillar.com/

- Technical concepts that are easy to appreciate and replicate.

One of the many challenges companies face is their ability to attract top-quality talent. As I type (Q3-23), many stressors are conspiring to make the employment marketplace challenging and febrile. The COVID-19 pandemic changed how many people view work. The concept of a 'job for life' with a company viewed as a 'safe employer' has fallen by the wayside. Many employees who adopted hybrid working during the pandemic want to maintain that lifestyle. There doesn't appear to be an easy fix to the increased costs companies are facing arising from Russia's invasion of Ukraine. Both the UK and EU employment markets continue to suffer the after-effects of Brexit. All this, and more, makes hiring new staff difficult.

So what has Caterpillar done to make itself more attractive to prospective employees?

Go to the main Caterpillar website, to be found at https://www.caterpillar.com. click on "Careers" in the top navigation, and you'll end up looking at a screen similar to that in Figure 2-1.

Figure 2-1: The main careers page of the website, reached by selecting "careers" in the top navigation.

Here's the structure of the URL:

Caterpillar.com/en/careers

Which follows the model:

Main site/language/page

The main point this tells us is we are looking at a webpage called "careers" belonging to the "caterpillar.com" domain. (Clearly, the structure also allows for different languages, but let's keep it simple for the moment.) The guiding principle is that page names *follow* the main site name, e.g. https://my-domain.com/page-name.

In the header—just under the main navigation—there's a nice text reinforcement, reminding site users where they are: Caterpillar > Careers.

Scroll a little way down the careers page and you arrive at Figure 2-2.

Figure 2-2: Main choices on the Caterpillar careers page. Click on "SEARCH FOR JOBS" to follow the example in the text.

The design highlights the main choices. To follow along you want to click "SEARCH FOR JOBS" and you'll arrive at Figure 2-3, where the magic starts.

Figure 2-3: The careers section of Caterpillar's website. Notice (a) the format change in the URL, and (b) the invitation for users to "JOIN THE COMMUNITY".

Study the URL: notice the changed format? That's highly significant and illustrates a clever approach to structuring websites. You ought to be familiar with this, as it can provide neat solutions to business challenges. You'll hear your IT colleagues talk about it and I want you to join their conversations confidently. What's the label for this? "Subdomains."

The What and Why of Subdomains

Subdomains are like the watertight bulkheads in a ship. You use a subdomain to create a separate section of your website—

which can then be used to host a specific type of content or to target a specific audience. It's like creating a separate room or space within a larger building, where you can display different products or services, or provide a specific type of experience for your website users.

For example, suppose your company website sells both consumer products (B2C) and business-to-business (B2B) services. You could use a subdomain to create a separate section of your website that is specifically targeted to your B2B customers, with content and services tailored to their needs. This could include information that helps businesses make informed purchasing decisions (for example, white papers, case studies, explanatory videos).

I introduced subdomains by likening them to a ship's watertight bulkheads, i.e. nothing can get through. This characteristic is a double-edged sword.

One advantage of subdomains is that they can use different technology to the main website. I use this characteristic in my own business.

Figure 2-4: You can use subdomains to house systems created with different technology to the main website.

I have various surveys and assessments for client use, all created with specialist software that's very different from the software used to create the main website. I host the surveys in a subdomain of my company website. When I email survey links to clients, they see my domain name and can have confidence in the link. Subdomains can use different technology or infrastructure, while still being associated with a main website.

This 'watertight bulkhead' feature means subdomains have another characteristic you ought to know about (and which you might not consider so useful). Search engines view subdomains as being distinct and separate entities from the parent domain. Because of this, any search engine optimization work you perform on the main domain remains there: it does *not* pass through to the subdomain. This is not necessarily a bad thing—but it is something you need to be aware of.

Should You Create More Webpages or a Subdomain?

Suppose you have new content to put online. Should it go into new webpages, or into a subdomain? Here are some considerations to review with your colleagues in the IT department:

Purpose

Does the new content expand the scope of the current website, or add new material, separate from the existing content? Do you expect your *existing* visitors (see below) to be interested in the new material?

Target audience

If your new content is written for a new audience, then creating a subdomain may make sense, in that it can be tailored to the needs of the new audience. If your new content is for your existing audience, then keeping it with the existing content makes sense, as it can benefit from SEO work already undertaken.

Technical requirements

If the new content requires different technology, software, or hosting than the existing site, using a subdomain makes sense. (See my example above, regarding the software I use for client surveys.) If you can add the new content to the existing site without major changes, then there's no real reason for complicating life unnecessarily.

Search engine optimization (SEO)

Already covered above: it's easier to enhance your SEO work by putting your new content onto pages on the main domain. If you create a subdomain, you are, in effect, starting a new SEO campaign.

Branding

If your new content is closely related to the existing site and brand, it makes sense to create new pages on the existing site. If you're creating a new brand identity, then a subdomain—or entirely new website—might be a better solution.

Caterpillar's "Careers" Subdomain

Clicking on "Jobs" from within the careers subdomain takes you to a searchable list of current jobs, similar to Figure 2-5.

Figure 2-5: Part of a job posting, showing the high level of detail that's available, including links to similar jobs.

When you see the level of detail that Caterpillar makes available, you can appreciate why it makes sense to have all the careers information gathered in its own subdomain, separate from the company's principal activity of building earth-moving equipment.

Other design features I admire are:

1. The simple and consistent design of the calls-to-action (black text in yellow rectangles)

2. The black and yellow combination is both highly effective and also consistent with Caterpillar's corporate brand

3. The design that keeps the calls-to-action towards the top of the page (reducing scrolling)

4. The simple way of differentiating the primary and secondary calls-to-action by simply changing the size of the buttons

5. The easy-to-hand share buttons for sharing job opportunities on social media, or with friends

There's much to admire in the simplicity of this site—and look at the level of detail they communicate about each job. This is a well-designed site, that's clearly come from close work by both IT and HR. A first class job—although, we're not finished yet: read on.

Applying for a job

If you click the "Apply Now" button in Figure 2-5, you end up at Figure 2-6.

Figure 2-6: Applying for a job moves you from Caterpillar's careers subdomain to a new environment, corporately branded, and built for Caterpillar by a Workday, a specialist software systems supplier.

The URL for the page in Figure 2-6 is:

https://cat.wd5.myworkdayjobs.com/CaterpillarCareers/...

As you're an expert at subdomains now, you'll be able to decode this with ease. What can you deduce?

A few minutes with Google and you find out that "myworkdayjobs" belongs to Workday[3], an enterprise software company with headquarters in California. The suffix at the start of the URL (cat. wd5.) tells us we are looking at a subdomain of "myworkdayjobs". A few more moments with Google, reveals that Workday use "myworkdayjobs" to advertise their own jobs:

https://workday.wd5.myworkdayjobs.com/Workday

Caterpillar's IT and HR staff have done an excellent job with the home they have created for their job opportunities. They have then expanded that by bringing in a specialist company to help them with the whole online application process—all corporately branded and presented to the user as a seamless experience.

But what about the invitation to "JOIN THE COMMUNITY" (Figures 2-3 and 2-5)? Remember that? What happens if you click that button? You end up at Figure 2-7.

The sign-up screen for Caterpillar's Talent Community is provided by Beamery, another specialist software supplier. Beamery offers "talent lifecycle management" and their website tells us that their "Beamery Digital" service is, "Here to help you optimize your employer brand and value proposition and rollout a Career Site you can be proud of".

3   https://workday.com

Figure 2-7: The sign-up page for Caterpillar's Talent Community, which runs on software from Beamery, another specialist software systems supplier.

It will surely come as no surprise to learn that Beamery also counts Workday among its clients. It's a small world.

The URL for joining Caterpillar's Talent Community is:

https://flows.beamery.com/caterpillarinc/...

From studying the URL you can see similarities with Workday's approach:

- You're looking at a subdomain of the beamery.com website (called, "flows"), and

- Within that subdomain, you're looking at a page called "caterpillarinc".

Figure 2-8 shows you an overall schematic of these various subdomains and systems.

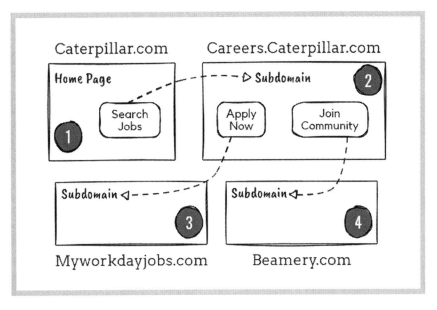

Figure 2-8: A schematic showing the major elements of the Caterpillar HR portal.

Box 1 in the top left of Figure 2-8 represents Caterpillar's corporate website. Visitors clicking on careers/job-related buttons are taken to the dedicated careers subdomain (Box 2). This keeps the corporate website clear for the huge amount of information the company wants to communicate about its major activities.

Potential candidates also have a well-designed 'mini-site' that allows them to easily research all the job opportunities available in the Caterpillar world.

Specialist software supplied by Workday processes job applications (Box 3). Anyone wanting to stay in touch with Caterpillar can register their details and interest using another application (Box 4) supplied by Beamery.

An impressive aspect of this multisystems design is the consistent branding across the various platforms. This is an enterprise-scale solution and has clearly benefited from a big budget. However, the basic approach of using subdomains combined with specialist suppliers is one that companies of all sizes could use. What's also clear is that *this solution was created by a team of experts working for the good of the entire corporation and not a single department working in isolation.*

I hope your organization will be able to benefit from Caterpillar's subtle and ingenious approach. While you've got your thinking cap on, I'd like to tell you about two other important ways in which systems can interact: *webhooks* and *application programming interfaces* (API). You'll hear these terms used by techy-folk and if you understand the fundamental differences, you'll have a better chance of ensuring your business needs are being well addressed.

Passing Data Between Systems

The Caterpillar case study shows how it's possible to present different systems in a user-friendly way. But what about the data *within* each system—how does that get passed between the systems, so the needs of the business are met? You might believe this to be a purely technical issue, of significance to IT folk alone. Mostly true, but a quick analogy will equip you to better quiz the developers and make sure your needs are met.

Imagine you own a general store in a small town, a typical corner shop that sells bread and milk, canned vegetables, bleach and bin liners—you get the picture. The shop is open six days a week. You're on site three days a week and work from home doing admin on the other days. You have two employees, Sue and John, who take turns staffing the shop when you're in your home office.

Sue and John are very different characters. Both are trustworthy, reliable, and do excellent work, but in very different ways. John was your first employee, and early on, you came to realize that if you didn't ask any questions, you didn't get any information. Sue joined your small team a year later and from day one, was much more forthcoming.

When John's minding the shop, you have to call him twice a day to find out what's going on. The strange thing is that he always seems mildly surprised to hear from you, even though you've made similar calls on many previous occasions. Your conversations follow the same format: how's the footfall? What are the approximate takings over the counter? Any returns or complaints? Any stock shortage issues? Eventually, you knock up a simple spreadsheet and email it to John twice a day. It's always returned, duly completed, within 20 minutes. There's no doubt that John always has the data to hand, but you can't help thinking, *'Wouldn't it be nice if he contacted me, rather than me having to chase him?'*

Sue's cut from different cloth. From her first day on duty, your phone rang whenever a customer returned an item for a refund. The moment a sale led to minimum stock levels being reached: your phone rang. You got a bit fed up with the multiple phone calls, but you always knew the current state of affairs.

What's going on and why does it matter?

John's acting like an *api* and Sue's acting like a *webhook*.

An *application programming interface* is an intermediate system that allows two different applications to exchange information. For example:

[System-A] requests [stock-level] from [System-B]

In the example, you're System-A and John is System-B. When John gets your email, he collects the relevant data, completes the spreadsheet and emails it back to you. No request from you = no action by John.

By contrast, a *webhook* is an automated message that's triggered by an event. So, when that customer bought two cans of paint, it resulted in four remaining on the shelf. Scanning the shelf, Sue counted the four remaining cans and realized the re-order level had been reached: her *webhook* kicked in and she phoned you.

Neither way of working is perfect, they're just different. When you're working with John, you have to keep polling him for information. If you forget to poll him, he'll just lock up the shop at the end of the day and go home. On the other hand, Sue volunteers information, but only when specific events trigger her to take action. If the event isn't in her lexicon, she'll just crack on with her day job.

Any solution implemented via an api will need coding. That takes time and needs testing, as do all coding jobs. (The testing is akin to the way you had to check the formulas in the spreadsheet you created as a go-between for you and John.) Time is money, so expect solutions using an api to be costly.

Webhooks, on the other hand, come ready-made. They comprise a predefined message (referred to as the *payload*) sent to a unique URL. You just have to be there, at that URL, ready to receive. From an IT perspective, that's way easier than messing around with programming interfaces. No polling is required, because the moment a triggering event happens, the message is sent. Solutions implemented using webhooks are quicker and easier (and therefore cheaper) to implement than those that need to communicate via an api.

If you find yourself in discussion about how different systems need to exchange data, check your business needs carefully. If you can satisfy them using webhooks, then you can expect to get a working system implemented quicker and cheaper than having to connect the systems via their programming interfaces.

You're now armed with some decent checklists and have clarity over some website-related terms you might come across. You should have increased confidence in your ability to engage in semi-technical conversations with your IT colleagues.

Coming up in Part B is an alternative way to consider your website and one that might appeal more to your business background. What if your website was an employee? If that were the case, it would surely have a formal job description. Turn the page to read what that might be.

Part B

Your Website as an Employee

3.

Is Your Website the Employee of the Decade?

I yor's story is a helpful starting point. The bright-eyed youngster recently started a new job at consulting engineers, Wicket Fase and Quick. He's as keen as mustard and delighted by the welcoming attitude of the WFQ staff. During his first week, Iyor meets three important department heads: Mary, Fiona, and Tony, and commits to helping each of them as best he can.

Mary leads the appointment-setting team. The team's job is to qualify leads produced by the marketing department, and—if appropriate—set up a meeting with a consulting engineer.

The Head of Engineering is Fiona Quick, and she's happiest when the office is empty. An empty office means Fiona's engineers are on the road, visiting potential clients.

Keeping Mary's appointment-setters fed with potential leads is the job of Tony Fase, Head of Marketing. Occasionally, Tony's colleagues unearth a lead that's so well qualified they pass it straight to Fiona's team.

Iyor spends his first month bouncing between these teams, taking in all the new processes and trying to remember everyone's names. He loves the excitement of his new job and is bursting with enthusiasm when he meets his friends Serge and 'G' for a drink after work. They are delighted Iyor is having such a great time, and are happy to learn about his new job and the work culture of

WFQ. Impressed with the progress their friend is making, Serge and G both offer introductions to their network of contacts and associates. Iyor is very grateful for his friends' help and promises to report progress when they all meet again.

At next month's meeting, Iyor reveals some impatience with his new colleagues at WFQ. He was hoping to have news for Serge and G on the introductions they had made, but neither the marketing department nor Mary's appointment-setting team had any news. Although frustrated at not being able to report substantial progress, other events added to Iyor's feeling of irritation.

"It's great getting to meet everyone, in all the different departments," he said, "But I feel homeless. I don't really belong to any one department—they just pass me around between them. I know they want me to understand how the whole organization works, but I want to feel like I belong. Right now, it's as if I'm watching it from the outside, through a slightly foggy window."

We'll leave Iyor and his friends to their drinks, while I tell you more about them. Iyor's family name is Ouebcitte, and Serge believes his family name, en Jinn, to be ancient Dutch.

Said aloud, you'll notice Iyor Ouebcitte sounds like *your website* and Serge en Jinn like *search engine*. When I tell you the enigmatic G's family name is 'Oogle', you'll see through my thinly veiled story. Let me give you some context.

Kicking off a project to build a new website has the excitement of any new business project, such as moving offices or opening a new store. The office move and store opening differ from the website project in a frequently overlooked and hugely important way.

The office move project ends when all the employees have moved into the new office. The store-opening project ends when the mayor cuts the ribbon and declares the new store open. In both these cases, the end of one project triggers the start of others. For example, now the new offices are occupied, they need to be maintained. Now the shop is open, stock levels need constant attention. One doesn't need expertise in retail or office logistics to appreciate these points: they seem intuitively obvious.

I have met countless clients who have abandoned the above logic when involved in website-creation projects. Once it's online, their focus moves elsewhere: their timing could hardly be worse. *Business websites have to work for a living, from the moment they are online.*

We all know "puppies aren't just for Christmas" and neither are websites. Both need constant attention, training (SEO optimization) and feeding (fresh content).

Iyor is greeted enthusiastically, but over time his new work colleagues seem to forget about him. They appear to be unclear what his job is and how he could help them do theirs better. Iyor's powerful connections with Serge and G remain untapped. I'm sure that if you saw this happening to a new recruit, you'd jump in and offer to help. I've seen websites suffer from this lack of 'ownership' and help wasn't as forthcoming as it ought to have been.

So what if your website were an employee? How would it fare?

Your Website as an Employee

Consider your website as a company employee. One who works 24/7, never takes a day off, and is available to customers all over the world. Just like a physical employee, your website has a job to do, and that will vary depending on their precise role. That said, all employees should behave according to the same principles: to represent the company in the best possible way and help customers find the information they need.

Think of your website as the front desk or receptionist—that first point of contact for many customers and visitors, and one that sets the tone for the entire experience they'll have with your business. A good website should be professional, helpful, and easy to interact with, just like a good employee.

Your website should be knowledgeable about your products or services, just like an employee who is an expert in their field. It should be able to answer questions, provide information, and guide customers to solutions that are the best for them. Your website should also be friendly and personable, in the same way you'd expect a good employee to be welcoming and approachable.

But your website is more than a receptionist. It could also be a salesperson, a marketer, or a customer service representative. Your website can help you generate leads, sell products or services, and provide support to customers. It can collect feedback and data that can help you improve your business.

So, just like you would carefully select and train a physical employee to represent your company, you should invest in your website and make sure it's doing its job effectively.

Investing in your website means putting in the time, effort, and resources to ensure that your website is both *functional* in IT terms and *effective* in achieving your business goals. Some companies stop at the *functional* work and I'm never quite sure why. Perhaps it's because the website belongs to IT, and nobody feels up to challenging that arrangement? Perhaps it's because business managers are too busy to have thought more deeply about what the website could do for their part of the business? I'll dig into these questions later, but for the moment here are several ways to invest in your website to ensure that it's doing its job effectively:

Regular updates and maintenance: Just like any other technology, your website requires regular updates and maintenance to ensure that it's functioning properly. This includes updating software and security protocols, fixing broken links and images, and optimizing website speed and performance. Clearly, these jobs belong to the IT department.

User experience optimization: Your website should be easy to use and navigate, with clear calls-to-action and user-friendly design. Investing in user-experience optimization can help ensure that your website is providing a positive experience for your visitors and helping them find what they're looking for quickly and easily. I'd expect your colleagues in IT to own this and manage it. However, it's likely that IT will need help from one or more business functions to help map out how users are expected to interact with the website and what the specific calls-to-action are, etc.

Search engine optimization (SEO): SEO is the label given to the set of tasks that help your website rank higher in search engine results pages (SERP). Investing in SEO can help ensure your website is visible to potential customers searching for the products or services you offer. It increases website traffic and ultimately drives more business. SEO is worthy of more discussion, and I revisit it in Chapter 4.

Content marketing: Investing in content marketing involves creating high-quality, relevant, and valuable content that resonates with your target audience. This can include blogposts, videos, infographics, and other types of content that provide value to your visitors and help build trust and authority for your brand. There is a clear relationship with SEO—more in Chapter 4.

Website analytics and data tracking: Investing in website analytics and data tracking can help you gain insights into how your website is performing and how visitors are interacting with your content. This data can help you make informed decisions about how to optimize your website and improve its effectiveness. For this to be successful, departments need to work together, with business departments defining the metrics and what data they need, and the IT department collecting it and compiling the reports.

Your Website's Job Description

Imagine your company's website was a regular employee, just like you. If so, it would have a job description. Try this for size.

Job Title: Company Website

Job Summary: The company website represents the company online and should provide an easily navigable, useful, and positive experience for visitors. The website works closely with other members of the team to develop and execute projects that support the company's business goals.

Responsibilities:

• Provide a positive experience for visitors, representing the company online.

• Showcase the company's products, services, and brand in a visually appealing and user-friendly manner.

• Ensure that the website and its content are optimized for search engines and easily discoverable by potential customers.

• Host valuable content such as blogposts, videos, and infographics that help build trust and authority for the brand.

- Capture visitor information and facilitate lead generation for the company.

- Track website analytics and provide data to help the team make informed decisions about website optimization and improvements.

- Ensure the website is up to date with the latest security protocols and that all software and plugins are regularly updated.

- Work closely with other members of the team to ensure the website aligns with overall marketing and branding efforts.

Qualifications:

- Strong understanding of website design, development, and optimization.

- Knowledge of content marketing and SEO best practices.

- Experience with website analytics and data tracking.

- Attention to detail and ability to manage multiple projects simultaneously.

Including qualifications might seem irrelevant when talking about a website, but I want to make a point: organizations expect employees to manage and check their own work, to some degree at least. A website can't really do this, so it has to rely on its human overseers to keep it on the straight and narrow. Keeping this in mind while reviewing the qualifications raises some interesting topics, worthy of thought and debate.

Website design: You'd rightly expect your IT colleagues to take the lead.

Content marketing and SEO: This is less obvious. Is content owned by Sales, Marketing, or IT (among others)? Are the required skills in-house or hired from an agency or freelancer? You should know the answers and be happy with them, as work done here will directly impact the ability of the site to support the business.

Website analytics: Similar to above. Who owns the tools? What are they? What access or reports can you expect? How will they help your department perform better?

Thinking about your company's website as if it were a real person and valued team member helps ensure it doesn't get side-lined or forgotten.

Coming chapters consider websites as employees within various specialized functions, important to all businesses. Here are some generic considerations to help business departments get the most from their company website. I expand on this list with specific examples in the chapters that follow.

1. Identify clear goals the website should achieve.

2. Understand the audience: Know your target audience and understand their needs, preferences, and behaviour.

3. Provide high-quality content: Create high-quality and engaging content that speaks to the needs and interests of the target audience. Use multiple media and keep content up-to-date and relevant.

4. Focus on the user experience, making it user-friendly and easily navigable.

5. Ensure content is optimized for search engines.

6. Monitor and analyze performance, using reports to make data-driven decisions.

Clearly, applying this list effectively will only be possible if the various business departments cooperate closely with the IT department. (Part C helps you do this.)

Search Engine Optimization (SEO)

Search Engine Optimization comes up a lot, both in this book and on client projects. Here are some general comments, ahead of the role-based chapters.

While SEO is a specialized skill that requires training and experience, non-IT managers can still play an important role in ensuring that their company's website is well optimized. For example, you could work with the IT team to help them structure the website in a way that makes it easy for search engines to crawl and index it. You can also work with content creators to help them use relevant keywords in a way that's applicable to your business and relevant to your visitors.

While you may not have the technical skills to execute all aspects of SEO, you can still provide valuable input and direction to the IT and content teams. For example, suppose your company wants to launch a new product line and wants to create a dedicated section of the website for the new product. The product manager can help the IT team identify relevant keywords to target, check proposed content is high-quality and valuable to users, and promote the new section through social media and other channels.

In summary, the business departments should maintain a keen interest in their content (if not be directly responsible for it). The same would hold true if a new brochure was being created. The use of online technology shouldn't, of itself, change anything.

4.

Your Website as a Marketing Assistant

Generating leads is a core marketing activity. So, if your website were your new Marketing Assistant, how would its job description read?

Job Title: Marketing Assistant (Website)

The Marketing Assistant (Website) supports the company's marketing efforts by increasing website traffic and generating leads. The website works closely with other members of the team to develop and execute a strategy that supports the company's business goals.

Responsibilities:

- Attract website traffic via multiple channels, such as social media, email marketing, and digital advertising.

- Optimize website structure and content for search engines to increase organic traffic and visibility.

- Host valuable content such as blogposts, videos, and infographics that attract potential customers and help to build trust and authority for the brand.

- Capture visitor information through various lead-generation techniques, such as pop-ups, forms, and gated content (lead magnets).

- Nurture leads through email marketing and other tactics to move them through the marketing funnel and convert them into customers.

- Analyze website and marketing data to identify trends and opportunities for improvement.

- Monitor and report on the success of various marketing campaigns and initiatives.

Qualifications:

- Strong understanding of digital marketing and lead-generation techniques.

- Knowledge of website design, development, and optimization.

- Experience with content marketing and SEO best practices.

- Proficiency in email marketing and marketing automation tools.

- Experience with website analytics and data tracking.

Use this Qualifications section as a checklist, to satisfy yourself that the team has access to all the required skills. (A similar list is included in each of the following chapters.)

To fulfill its Marketing Assistant role, the website needs to focus on attracting traffic, capturing leads, and nurturing those leads towards becoming customers. The following three points will help this.

Optimizing for search engines: Work that optimizes content for search engines shouldn't be done at the expense of human visitors—and nor does it need to be. High-quality content that is valuable to the website's target audience and well optimized for search engines satisfies both parties. Besides content, the website's structure and metadata should also be optimized for search engines. Other valuable SEO techniques include using internal links to satisfy typical user journeys and building extensive backlinks to improve the website's overall ranking.

Hosting valuable content: Blogposts, videos, and infographics can help attract potential customers, and build trust and authority for the brand. This content should be informative, engaging, and relevant to the website's target audience. By providing value through this content, the website can establish itself as a trusted resource in its industry. It's possible to write copy that will be appreciated equally by both real people and search engines.

Capturing visitor information: There are many ways of encouraging visitors to engage: sign-up forms, online chat, telephone callback, etc. The aim is to get visitors to provide their contact details in exchange for content or offers they find valuable.

By analyzing website and marketing data, you can identify trends and opportunities for improvement in your organization's online marketing strategy. It's a continuous process of refinement. Over time, it leads to higher quality traffic plus more and better leads.

You can help your new marketing assistant perform better by (a) attracting appropriate traffic and (b) directing it with a clear call-to-action, toward (c) a good lead magnet. Too many companies slip up on all these points, which explains their poor results: it's time to take a closer look.

Creating Valuable Website Content

Gaining trust online, demonstrating your expertise and verifying your authority are critical steps in turning website visitors into viable leads. Luckily, this is also Google's view. To help you achieve these objectives, Google introduced the E-A-T (Expertise, Authority, and Trustworthiness) concept in the 2014 edition of its Search Quality Guidelines[4] and has continued to give it increasing prominence.

In December 2022, Google announced a significant addition to E-A-T by adding an additional 'E', for 'experience'. The company also clarified the relationships between all four elements; Experience, Expertise, Authority, and Trustworthiness.

Even though it's not directly a ranking factor, E-E-A-T is very important to Google—and hence, to you too. Google has approximately 10,000 Search Quality Raters worldwide. They manually review the quality of webpages and their results are used to improve the search algorithms. The reviewers use the E-E-A-T guidelines to study:

- The content of the webpage under review

- The website to which the page belongs

- The creator of the content

4 The 2021 edition of Google's Search Quality Guidelines refers to E-A-T 137 times (in fewer than 200 pages).

This is what Google has told its Search Quality Raters about the addition of 'experience':

> "Consider the extent to which the content creator has the necessary first-hand or life experience for the topic. Many types of pages are trustworthy and achieve their purpose well when created by people with a wealth of personal experience. For example, which would you trust: a product review from someone who has personally used the product or a 'review' by someone who has not?"

Figure 4-1 shows how Google has emphasized the importance of Trust, by placing it at the centre of all four E-E-A-T elements. The company justified this move thus, "... untrustworthy pages have low E-E-A-T no matter how Experienced, Expert, or Authoritative they may seem."

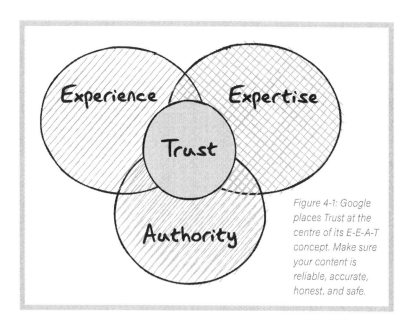

Figure 4-1: Google places Trust at the centre of its E-E-A-T concept. Make sure your content is reliable, accurate, honest, and safe.

As important as E-E-A-T is, it's vital to keep some perspective. It's too easy to come across misleading or incorrect information online. Some pundits have overegged the pudding and want you to believe that E-E-A-T is some newfangled way of ranking search results. It isn't. To keep you forewarned, here are some common misunderstandings. Whatever you may read online, there is no such thing as an 'E-E-A-T score' and E-E-A-T itself is not an algorithm. You cannot use E-E-A-T to fix technical weaknesses. E-E-A-T operates side-by-side with other optimization techniques, it doesn't render any of them obsolete.

There are additional points worth exploring in more detail: the effort you should give E-E-A-T and an expectation of what you'll get in return.

How much effort should you give E-E-A-T?

Google does not treat all websites the same but categorizes them according to an additional concept: 'Your Money or Your Life' (YMYL). Webpages aren't awarded a numeric YMYL score, more a low to high rating. E-E-A-T and YMYL go hand in hand and understanding where your business sits within the YMYL framework will help you decide how much effort you give E-E-A-T.

Content with high YMYL has the potential to affect a person's health, finances, happiness, or safety. Google's quality raters will hold such pages to a much higher E-E-A-T standard.

Some example content and its likely YMYL rating:

- *Pencil sketching for beginners*
  No YMYL rating

- *Celebrity gossip, entertainment news, sports*
  Low

- *Information about voting, social services, child custody, etc.*
  High

- *Pet health*
  High

- *Health & safety, medical issues, drugs, hospitals, etc.*
  Max

All ecommerce pages are high YMYL. So, if the owner of *pencil sketching for beginners* decides to sell courses online, the ecommerce pages will automatically have high YMYL, even though the main pages might not. This is a good example of where Google's quality raters would have to use their judgment.

The higher you think your YMYL rating will be, the more E-E-A-T effort you should put into your content.

What can you expect in return?

As E-E-A-T is not a direct ranking factor, its influence is more gradual. Building trust with users takes time, and it takes even more time for them to reflect that trust into your website—and yet more time for it to be picked up and acted on by search engines.

Take *pencil sketching for beginners* and assume the site is a 'hints & tips' site run by an enthusiast and has no ecommerce capabilities. The owner can share their expertise without being held accountable by Google's quality raters and E-E-A-T.

The owner upgrades the site and offers for sale a range of products: an online group course; weekend painting retreats; and a new 1-on-1 course; *Sketching for Advanced Artists*. This content falls under YMYL and Google will hold the content to a much higher E-E-A-T standard. For example, the quality raters might want to see clear evidence of delighted customers. They might also look more closely at the artist's biography: has the artist mentioned their membership of the Royal Academy and schooling at the world renowned Glasgow School of Art? And how about their residency at the Massachusetts Institute of Technology? Are there content or backlinks verifying these claims?

Clearly building such a site from a simple hints and tips site will take time. And it will then take more time for the search engines to index the new content, and for it to be verified.

If Google holds your content to a high E-E-A-T standard, then patience is the name of the game. Focus on the high quality that your clients would expect of you, and you'll also satisfy Google and improve your search results.

The highs and lows of E-E-A-T evaluations

Google's search quality rater guidelines are a useful reference source. Here's what the guidelines instruct raters to look for if they are considering a low E-E-A-T evaluation.

"Low quality pages often lack an appropriate level of E-E-A-T for the topic or purpose of the page. Here are some examples:

- The content creator lacks adequate experience, e.g. a restaurant review written by someone who has never eaten at the restaurant.

- The content creator lacks adequate expertise, e.g. an article about how to skydive written by someone with no expertise in the subject.

- The website or content creator is not an authoritative or trustworthy source for the topic of the page, e.g. tax form downloads provided on a cooking website.

- The page or website is not trustworthy for its purpose, e.g. a shopping page with minimal customer service information."

Conversely, here's the guidance for "high" and "very high" E-E-A-T evaluations.

"Pages with **High** E-E-A-T are trustworthy or very trustworthy. Experience is valuable for almost any topic. Social media posts and forum discussions are often High quality when they involve people sharing their experience. From writing symphonies to reviewing home appliances, first-hand experience can make a social media post or discussion page High quality."

"**Very high** E-E-A-T is a distinguishing factor for Highest quality pages. A website or content creator who is the uniquely authoritative, go-to source for a topic has very high E-E-A-T. A content creator with a wealth of experience may be considered to have very high E-E-A-T for topics where experience is the primary factor in trust. A very high level of expertise can justify a very high E-E-A-T assessment. Very high E-E-A-T websites and content creators are the most trusted sources on the internet for a particular topic."

Creating high-value E-E-A-T content is worth doing. However, it's a long game (so the sooner your new Marketing Assistant starts, the better).

Your Lead Magnets—WTF?

Weak target focus (WTF) is the most common reason for lead magnets to perform poorly. Before diving into the details of website-driven lead generation, let me set the scene with an introduction to lead magnets and sign-up forms.

The problem lead magnets solve

Most of your website visitors are not ready to buy. (There are a few exceptions and I address them shortly.) Lead magnets help plug the gap between the visitor who isn't ready to commit and the one who is.

What is a lead magnet?

Some form of gated content: material that visitors access in exchange for some contact details entered via a sign-up form (normally name and email address).

A good lead magnet can be the start of a fruitful client/supplier relationship. A good lead magnet serves two commanders equally: the website visitor and the website owner.

For the visitor, a lead magnet should help them solve an important (or urgent) need. The more personalized the help is to their circumstances, the more value they attribute to it and the greater the trust they will place in the website owner. Signing up for a lead magnet provides a low-risk avenue for a visitor to assess a potential supplier's capabilities. A good magnet should help answer the questions, "Do I like the cut of this person's jib? Can I trust them?"

For the company, the lead magnet is a chance to showcase their skill and help differentiate themselves from their competitors. It's an opportunity to provide honest advice, with the genuine intent of helping the visitor solve their immediate problem. This helps position visitors who might purchase at some future point. Website visitors understand that signing up for a lead magnet will not keep the website owner fed and watered—they're not expecting the entire answer for free.

Do all businesses need lead magnets?

The vast majority. The small number of businesses that can manage without share both these characteristics:

- They sell directly to consumers (B2C)

- Clients make an approach when their issue has reached some critical threshold

For example, my company manages the website of a clinical psychologist who fulfills these criteria and runs a successful practice without having a lead magnet. Clients find her website as the result of an internet search; either directly or by clicking a link on a referring website (such as Psychology Today). Some clients arrive via a recommendation from a friend or family member.

Regardless of how clients come to contact the psychologist, they do so because they've reached a point where they recognize they need help. People in this position don't need a lead magnet. Once they find a supplier they can trust (E-E-A-T again), they move quickly to implement the full solution.

To illustrate how circumstances could change, let's suppose the psychologist expanded her offerings (to include a workshop on mental health, for example) and started marketing to businesses (B2B). The purchasing decision is now very different: the workshop participant (who receives the benefit) is a different person from the one paying. It's highly likely that the purchasing decision would involve several people from different departments, for example, procurement, HR, training, and various other heads of department. With this level of complexity, the psychologist could increase her chances of closing the sale by having supporting material available to her corporate clients when she isn't. A lead magnet would be an important part of that supporting library.

In summary, lead magnets will be useful to all businesses operating in a B2B market and most businesses operating in a B2C environment.

Essential ingredients of a good lead magnet

The root of 'weak target focus' lies in the false belief that more is better. The frequently quoted argument is variations of, *"The more people sign up for my lead magnet, the bigger my email list, the greater my sales numbers."* This is faulty logic. Focus on quality over quantity.

A good lead magnet encourages the right people to sign up, while signaling that those outside your niche shouldn't bother. Achieve this by following the guidance in the next six subsections.

Clarify your target

Find the courage to be brave: be precise. Don't worry about excluding people. Reducing the size of the pond you're fishing in will feel counterintuitive at first but will yield results in the long run.

For example, legal and medical secretaries both have specialist skills that separate them from other secretarial or general administrative positions. If you focus on training legal and medical secretaries, your lead magnet should be useful to these specific groups, and by omission exclude people with more general secretarial skills. For example:

- *Take our test and discover whether you could handle the stress of being a medical secretary.* Good

- *Crush your next interview with our sample legal secretary interview questions.* Good

- *Improve your secretarial skills with our 10 point checklist.* WTF

The first two titles also tell your visitor that you know your onions. To create a good lead magnet that satisfies the first two titles, you must have done your research and know your market. By contrast, you could subcontract the third title to a general copywriter. While there's nothing inherently wrong with that, it's not going to attract your target market. What it will do is fill your email list with inferior quality leads—more on that later.

Be of service first

This is a subtle, but I believe important point. So far, few companies appear to have taken advantage of it, so the sooner you act, the better.

Here's an overview of the process underpinning a traditional lead magnet:

- The visitor arrives on a page advertising the lead magnet

- The page contains content that persuades the visitor to complete the form

- The visitor enters their contact details (typically name and email address) and clicks the 'complete' button

- The visitor is redirected to what's called the 'thank you' page. This contains information about how they can get their lead magnet. It might be available as a download directly from the 'thank you' page, or it might have been emailed to the address the visitor entered

For completeness, it's worth noting two additional points. Many countries now have legislation in place governing the collection of visitor details. Of course, you should comply with regulations. A common European standard is GDPR[5]. Some website owners use a two-step sign-up process. The first step is the website form. Completing this form triggers an email to the new registrant's email address. To complete their registration, the new registrant must click a link in this email. This two-step process ensures visitors use a genuine email address when signing up.

I don't want GDPR or the precise sign-up mechanism to cloud the main point, which is: Google cannot read all the great content in your lead magnet. In this example, your entire lead magnet is behind a sign-up form. Google's indexing bots will stop at the sign-up form (as will their human counterparts, Google's quality raters). So, no matter how good your lead magnet content is, it will only be available to visitors who sign up.

Second point; you're asking people to take you on trust. There has been an explosion of lead magnets in recent years and with that substantial variation in quality. Many visitors are shy about sharing their contact details.

One way to build trust is to deliver value free of any need to sign up. I take this approach with the Website Effectiveness Check (WEC)[6] offered on my website. The evaluation provides five percentage website effectiveness scores: an overall score and four detailed scores, each addressing a particular aspect of website effectiveness.

---

5   General Data Protection Regulation, https://gdpr.eu/
6   https://s.activepresence.com/website-evaluation

Try running the WEC against your own website, so you can experience the process firsthand. You can run the check without surrendering any contact details. On completion, the system clearly displays your overall score. At this point—having already provided some valuable information and (hopefully) proved my value—I ask you if you'd like to exchange your contact details for a detailed report, giving you the additional detailed scores. Up to that point, you can leave, free of any concern that I've put your details onto an email list.

From my perspective as a business owner, this gives me the opportunity to show my expertise and add real value to a visitor's business early in a potential relationship. If the visitor doesn't want to take it any further, that's fine: I'm saved the cost of storing contact details of someone who would never have become a client. The visitor leaves free from potential contact they didn't want. The best outcome for both parties. Visitors that sign up for the full report are showing interest in their business and trust in me. They get a detailed report they can use as the basis for an action plan, and I'm able to contact someone who's interested in my work. An excellent result for both parties.

Personalize the promise

The Website Effectiveness Check also shows how personalizing your lead magnet to your visitor's circumstances is an excellent way to show more expertise and build great trust. The more personal you can make the experience, the more you'll be helping your visitor and the easier you're making it for them to trust you.

For example, *Take our test and discover whether you could handle the stress of being a medical secretary*, suggests the user will get a personalized report giving them insights on how they might respond to the role. You can imagine this being valuable to someone considering training as a medical secretary. This personal score makes it more valuable than the second lead magnet, which offers the same sample interview questions to all users. If the second lead magnet also included an assessment of the responses to the interview questions, clearly its value would soar—but such capability makes it read more like a chargeable service than a lead magnet.

Demonstrate your respect for the value of your visitor's email address by offering something very specific in exchange.

Be clear about the key benefits

Be crystal clear about what's delivered and the benefits the user will get from the lead magnet. In the example of the *medical secretary stress test*, is the user getting an on-screen score, or an emailed report (or both)? If a report, how many pages? How was the test developed? How accurate and reliable are the results? Is the test recognized by any professional bodies? You get the picture.

Have a clear call-to-action

Button text is important. Joanna Wiebe, founder of Copyhackers, recommends: Have the headline and button in reasonable proximity to one another. Have the button text mirror the headline text. Compose the button text so it completes either of the following sentences:

- I want to...

- I want you to...

Applying this to the example of the sample interviews for the legal secretary, button texts could be:

- *I want to...* Crush My Next Interview

- *I want you to...* Show Me My Sample Questions

Demonstrate your credentials and position for purchase

Your lead magnet is the first substantial content you deliver to your visitor. It changes your visitor into a lead. That's all. It doesn't change them into a raving fan or someone who's going to hit your ecommerce system with their credit card until it melts.

Many businesses mess up here. Your new lead will certainly not share the enthusiasm you have for your topic. You're one of many plates they are trying to keep spinning on many sticks. They need your help, and your lead magnet must deliver it.

It's perfectly reasonable to show examples of how you've helped clients in similar circumstances. This helps build trust and shows your expertise. It's reasonable to tell them more about you, and the background to your work and approach (authority).

Save the sales pitch for when you've qualified your new lead and have something specific to offer.

Ditch the Dead Wood

A section on lead magnets would not be complete without a comment on the overall health of the email list to which leads are added.

Lead magnets based on questionnaires clearly collect more information about the leads. Expect fewer leads of higher quality. Visitors with a low level of interest won't bother completing an assessment: good—you don't want them, as they are a poor-quality lead. Visitors who do complete the questionnaire have shown enough commitment and interest to qualify themselves as a viable lead. In completing your questionnaire, they've also given you information you can use in further qualifying them.

We all have the continual challenge of clearing out the dead wood from our email list. That dead wood is our own fault. We've encouraged it over the years by offering generic information worth surrendering an email address for, even though that person had no intent of ever becoming a client.

Visitors have become savvier about how companies use their information. Many visitors provide email addresses they only use when seeking free content There are hundreds of thousands of email lists out there stuffed to the gills with duff emails—people who are never going to give you money or recommend you strongly to their network.

The email providers count this 'subscribed and disengaged' population within your overall subscriber count and are happy to hit your credit card every month on this basis. This does more damage than just unnecessarily inflating your expenses. Members of your list who are 'subscribed and disengaged' damage your email open rates and ultimately, your domain's sender reputation. You should ditch these people.

Focus on those who are engaged (i.e. those who read your emails) and ditch the rest. Alter your engagement strategy to encourage subscriptions from those who are more likely to be genuinely interested in what you offer. You're the expert in your market. You know what bugs people. You know what they're struggling with. Drive a truck full of value through that and see who flags you down.

Your Marketing Assistant might be doing a great job of generating qualified leads. But how good is your Sales Rep at converting them into customers? Turn the page and find out.

5.

Your Website as a Sales Representative

A website that behaves as a Sales Rep will use ecommerce to close sales. In the same way that marketers like to distinguish themselves from sales personnel, ecommerce sites differ from the lead-generation sites discussed in the previous chapter.

The Sales Representative (Website) specializes in converting leads into customers. The Marketing Assistant (Website)— discussed in the previous chapter—focuses on building brand awareness and generating interest. Frequently, in the offline world there is an overlap between marketing and sales roles, and the same can happen online. Both roles are important and complementary and you need both to create business growth.

Here's a job description to emphasize the sales representative role.

Job Title: Sales Representative (Website)

The Sales Representative (Website) should generate revenue. It converts leads into customers by providing information, guidance, and support throughout the sales process. The website works closely with other members of the sales team to develop and execute a strategy that supports the company's business goals.

Responsibilities:

- Engage with potential customers by providing valuable information about products and services.

- Provide guidance and support to customers throughout the sales process, including answering questions, addressing concerns, and facilitating transactions.

- Use techniques such as pop-ups, forms, and gated content to capture customer information.

- Nurture existing/previous customers via email marketing and other tactics, to move them through additional sales funnels and secure more sales.

- Collaborate with other members of the sales team to identify opportunities for cross-selling and up-selling.

- Analyze website and sales data to identify trends and opportunities for improvement.

- Monitor and report on the success of various sales initiatives.

- Stay up-to-date with the latest sales trends and best practices.

Qualifications:

- Strong understanding of sales and lead-generation techniques.

- Knowledge of website design, development, and optimization, with particular reference to ecommerce systems.

- Experience with lead nurturing and email marketing.

- Proficiency in website analytics and data tracking.

- Ability to provide exceptional customer service and support.

- Attention to detail and ability to manage multiple projects simultaneously.

There are three important categories of capability to examine when looking at ecommerce sites.

First, their ability to function effectively as a sales representative, by engaging with potential customers and guiding them through the sales process.

Second, their ability to understand the customer's needs and expand the sale to include items the customer might not have in mind (cross-selling and up-selling).

Third, the ability to make additional sales to existing/previous customers, by staying in touch and looking after them.

The second and third categories of activity can be hugely improved by analyzing website sales data. Good ecommerce systems come equipped with good sales-analysis systems, so be sure to dig into these, if you're considering an ecommerce upgrade.

Crossover between marketing and sales exists offline and online. Everything in the previous chapter about engagement, qualification, emails etc. also applies here. In this chapter, I want to focus on the differences between a (website) Marketing Assistant and Sales Rep.

The Marketing Assistant (Website) is focused on building brand awareness and generating interest in the company's products or services. It uses content marketing, social media, and other tactics to attract potential customers to the website and provide them with valuable information that positions the company as an expert in its field. It also uses lead-generation techniques to capture customer information. It moves potential customers further through the sales funnel by educating and nurturing them.

On the other hand, the Sales Representative (Website) is focused on converting leads into customers. It engages with potential customers by providing information about products and services, answering questions, and addressing concerns. The website acting as a sales representative uses lead-generation techniques to capture potential customer information and then works to move those leads through the sales funnel, using email marketing and other tactics to convert them into paying customers.

Important Ecommerce Functions

If you're implementing an ecommerce system, pay careful attention to the following important functions. Although they clearly have a strong IT flavour, they all have the potential to significantly impact your business, so dig deep and make sure you're happy about each of these points.

Product catalogue management

This addresses the organization and display of your products or services. A good product catalogue management system allows you to add, edit, and delete products easily, and organize them into categories and subcategories. This function is critical because it directly affects your customer's shopping experience, determining how easy it is for them to find and purchase what they are looking for.

Shopping cart and checkout

The shopping cart and checkout functions allow customers to add products to their cart, review their order, and complete the checkout process by providing payment and shipping information. These functions are critical because they are the final steps of the purchase process, and any friction or confusion at this stage can result in cart abandonment (more later) and lost sales.

Payment and order processing

The payment and order-processing function involves securely processing customer payments, verifying orders, and generating order confirmations and receipts. This function is critical because it directly affects revenue and cash flow, and any errors or delays in payment processing can lead to dissatisfied customers and lost sales.

Inventory management

This involves tracking and managing the availability and movement of the products or services you offer. This function is critical because it ensures that the business has adequate stock levels to fulfil customer orders and avoids overselling or underselling products.

Customer management

This addresses managing customer information, preferences, and interactions. A good customer management system will allow you to provide personalized shopping experiences, improve customer loyalty, and gather valuable insights into customer behaviour and preferences.

All these functions are essential for a successful ecommerce system. They directly impact your customers' shopping experiences, your company's revenue, and the overall success of the ecommerce platform.

Special Additional Shopping Cart Functions

First, to clarify terminology: 'ecommerce' refers to the whole process of selling online. 'Shopping cart' refers to the software (and processes) specifically associated with purchasing.

There are three aspects of shopping carts that attract wide attention and have the potential for significant business impact: abandoned cart, cross-selling, and up-selling. Here's a briefing on each.

Abandoned cart

The term 'abandoned cart' refers to those situations where a customer adds items to their online shopping cart but does not complete the purchase. The customer literally 'abandons' the cart before completing the checkout process.

Abandoned carts can occur for various reasons, such as unexpected shipping costs, a complicated checkout process, technical issues, or simply a change of mind. Clearly, abandoned carts are a significant concern for ecommerce businesses, as they indicate lost sales.

Is there anything you can do once a cart has been abandoned? Yes, all is not lost. Many businesses will send cart abandonment emails to remind customers of their unfinished purchase. Of course, you can only do this, if you know your customer's email address. For this reason, many shopping cart systems collect customer information in (at least) two stages—making a point of collecting the customer's name and email address first, so that contact can still be made, should the purchase fail. Some cart abandonment email sequences can be automated and include incentives (such as discounts or free shipping) to encourage customers to complete their purchase.

Cross-selling and up-selling

Cross-selling and up-selling are two marketing techniques used to encourage customers to purchase additional products or upgrades.

Cross-selling refers to offering customers complementary or related products to the one they are already buying. The goal is to increase the customer's overall purchase value and improve the shopping experience by suggesting other products they might be interested in. For example, if a customer is buying a camera, cross-selling would be offering them a camera bag or a memory card that goes with the camera.

Up-selling, on the other hand, refers to suggesting an upgraded or more expensive version of the product the customer is interested in buying. The goal is to increase the average order value and potentially boost revenue by encouraging customers to purchase a higher-priced item. For example, if a customer is interested in buying a basic laptop, up-selling would be suggesting a laptop with more features and higher specifications.

Cross-selling and up-selling are not mutually exclusive. The similarities between them are that both techniques aim to increase the customer's purchase value and improve the overall shopping experience. Additionally, both techniques require an understanding of the customer's needs and preferences to make relevant product suggestions.

The differences between cross-selling and up-selling lie in the type of products being offered and the goal of the technique.

Cross-selling has a focus on complementary or related products, while up-selling suggests a higher-priced or upgraded product. The aim of cross-selling is to increase the customer's overall purchase value, while up-selling aims to increase the average order value.

Examples of cross-selling include offering customers a phone case when they purchase a new phone, suggesting a matching tie when customers buy a suit, or recommending a moisturizer when customers purchase a skincare product. Examples of up-selling include offering customers a more powerful computer processor when they are buying a new computer, suggesting a premium subscription package for a streaming service, or recommending a luxury watch instead of a basic one.

Ecommerce Starting Point

Even modest ecommerce implementations can evolve into complex projects. If your company is implementing ecommerce, I'm sure your IT colleagues will have a solid plan in place. However, you should check the following, to make sure the needs of the business (and your company's customers) are well represented.

Goals and objectives

The IT department will focus on technical issues and milestones. You can add value to the project by ensuring the business-related issues are looked after well. For example, is the target market clearly defined and well understood? Does the team know what products or services are to be sold? Are there specific sales targets?

Make sure your project covers the following:

1. Identify the target market, including demographics such as age, gender, income level, and geographic location.

2. Analyze your competitors' ecommerce websites, examining their strengths and weaknesses. Apart from pricing and products, examine the user experience in detail.

3. Set specific sales targets, identifying desired revenue and profit margins, and targets for the first year of operation.

4. Define your product or services, documenting unique selling points or competitive advantages.

5. Clarify your marketing strategy, including the channels you intend using to reach your target audience (for example, social media, email marketing, and online advertising).

6. Check that the budget covers both implementing and promoting your ecommerce system. This includes allocating funds for website development, hosting, payment processing, and marketing.

Ecommerce platform research

I've come across ecommerce projects where the skills of the implementation team dictated the platform choice. The needs of the business were not paramount in the decision. Do your own research and look for a platform that you believe meets the business needs, as opposed to the path of least (IT) resistance.

Website development and user experience

Although your IT colleagues will take the lead here, you should make sure what's developed is visually appealing, easy to navigate, and optimized for search engines. The user experience should be intuitive, with a simple checkout process and clear calls-to-action.

Integration of payment and shipping options

From a business perspective, give careful consideration to payment gateways and shipping options. For example, you may have pre-existing retail relationships that you can expand to serve your new online shop.

Common Ecommerce Errors

Implementing a new ecommerce system is a complex and challenging project. Many companies make some oversights along the way. To give you a head start on your own project, here are some of the most serious ecommerce implementation mistakes I've come across.

Inadequate planning

All ecommerce projects I've come across have taken longer to implement than initially planned. Getting support from an ecommerce-experienced Project Manager is money well spent, in my opinion. Delays and cost overruns will end up costing you more than developing a decent plan in the first instance.

One of the common planning-related errors I've come across is not leaving enough time for product photography. To illustrate the point, look at any online store selling watches. All carry an extensive range, with many models for both men and women. Each watch will have multiple photographs, and sometimes, videos. Creating the photography is a huge subproject. Even when done, all the different images have to be assembled into an online catalogue and uploaded into the ecommerce database. The time required for photography is commonly underestimated (and time is money, of course).

Poor user experience

Ecommerce platforms that are difficult to use or navigate lose sales and lead to dissatisfied customers. Check for an intuitive and user-friendly experience.

Also, be on the lookout for long load times and an unnecessarily complex or long purchase sequence. Time and money spent on user testing in this area is a wise investment.

Insufficient security

Ecommerce platforms process sensitive customer information, making security a critical issue. We've all read the stories in the press, where a data breach has led to loss of customer trust, and potential legal liabilities. A major UK institution—the Royal Mail—had all its international deliveries blocked for over a month in early 2023. The LockBit cartel, infamous in IT security circles, claimed responsibility for the 'distributed denial of service' attack. Responsibility for security clearly lies within the IT department (for example, the use of HTTPS protocol, secure sockets layer (SSL) encryption, and two-factor authentication to protect customer information). However, you have a responsibility too, in ensuring that your colleagues accessing the internals of the ecommerce system practice good 'security hygiene' (so no leaving your password on sticky notes, tacked to the bottom of the screen).

Poor integration

Ecommerce platforms generate revenue and customers, the very life blood of businesses. It stands to reason that your ecommerce needs to be able to pump that blood throughout the business. Their success at doing so lies in their ability to integrate with other business systems, such as inventory management, order processing, accounting, customer relationship management, outbound email, etc.

Imagine what could happen if your ecommerce site's inventory wasn't integrated with the main inventory management system. Online customers might end up placing orders your company couldn't deliver. Each of us can imagine many difficult situations. Your IT colleagues will look to you for your experience of the business processes in your area. Give deep thought to where all the data flows and draw as many diagrams as you can to account for everything you can think of. Ecommerce tentacles spread wide and deep. Focusing on researching and documenting them is time well spent.

Inadequate testing

Testing budgets always get close scrutiny. "Do we really need to do that much?" Yes, you do. "Technology is so much more reliable nowadays?" True. People aren't.

A real-life example I witnessed: a company exhibiting at an industry conference made a last-minute decision to offer a discount to people who purchased on the day (from their exhibition stand). Ecommerce discount codes were created and emailed to the stand staff. A few minutes later a panic text message was sent to many phones: *Help: the discount codes don't work!* The situation was resolved promptly by a switched-on member of the IT department who (correctly) guessed that the codes had been applied to the wrong category of products. But, here's the point: it would have taken the original developers less than two minutes to process a dummy order and uncover their error. The codes were created and sent on their way, with a fundamental question unanswered: *do they work?*

A mantra from my days at IBM: "If it isn't tested, it doesn't work." Be clear with your IT colleagues as to specific business functions that you expect to see formally tested. Ask to see the test plan. Volunteer to help with its creation and collecting the results. (More on testing in Chapter 9.)

Inadequate training

As ecommerce reaches every nook and cranny, it frequently creates the need for special training. "But we've never had to do a single shipment of three tee-shirts and a grass mower to Norway before." Online customers will test you and your processes to breaking point. Cover as many eventualities as you can think of. Select staff for special training to become 'power users', so they can help others keep the business moving. Above all else, make it easy for customers to give you their money.

Lack of software maintenance

This is one for your IT colleagues. Just be aware that ecommerce platforms require ongoing maintenance and updates to ensure they remain functional and secure. As they link to so many different systems, their maintenance requirements may seem more frequent and involved than other systems you're used to.

Ignoring/not collecting customer feedback

This is closely aligned with the comment on testing. It stands to reason that your ecommerce system has to be customer focused to be successful. Have a budget for collecting, processing, and acting on customer feedback.

Avoiding these oversights can help you implement a successful ecommerce system that delivers a positive customer experience, increases revenue, and supports business growth.

It's time to consider other roles websites can perform that also help deliver an organization's overall experience, albeit not directly associated with revenue generation. For example, training.

6.

Your Website as an In-House Trainer

Generating *leads* and *revenue* are major reasons for a company to want an effective website. Both align with Peter Drucker's profound observation that, "The purpose of a business is to create and keep a customer." Of course, there are also other important support roles. Some are external facing (e.g. customer support) and others internal (e.g. human resources). There is a third category that brackets both the internal and external environments, such as training (and in a wider sense, learning management systems).

This chapter uses training as a vehicle for reviewing the website capabilities you should expect in support systems. If your interest is human resources, you won't find a better exemplar than the Caterpillar case study, reviewed in Chapter 2.

Learning Management Systems

Everything I've mentioned previously about planning properly, understanding users' needs, etc. still applies. I use this chapter to call out additional items you should attend to regarding support roles and training in particular.

The Learning Management System (LMS) sector has exploded in recent years, in both the number of systems available and their capabilities. Here's an introduction to the features you should be looking for in a modern, capable LMS.

Course creation and management tools

The ability to create and organize courses, modules, lessons, and quizzes, and to manage course materials, assignments, and student progress.

This is the heart of any LMS. You should expect a user-friendly course-creation interface that enables instructors and course creators to create, organize, and publish course content easily. This should include the ability to upload or create multimedia content (videos, images, and audio), and create interactive elements, such as quizzes, polls, and assessments.

Course schedules

You should also be able to create course schedules, lesson plans, and assignments. (More on grading assignments and tracking student progress later.) Course scheduling should address setting start and end dates, creating the course structure, and scheduling specific lessons or topics to be covered on specific dates. This gives students a clear understanding of what will be covered and when.

Lesson plans

Instructors should be able to create lesson plans that outline the learning objectives, instructional methods, and assessment strategies for each lesson or topic. This ensures courses are well organized, with a clear focus on what students need to achieve and how they will be evaluated.

Drip feed of course content

Drip feeding course content refers to the delivery of course content in predefined segments, according to a set of rules. Instead of giving students access to all the course content at once, the course materials are 'drip-fed' in smaller, manageable chunks.

Not all systems have this capability, so if it's important to you, carefully check the capability on offer. The rules governing the drip-feed system may be a simple time-based rule, or something more configurable.

Example of a time-based rule: a course designed to run for eight weeks with a drip-feed schedule that releases new content each week. Students have access to the new material regardless of their progress with previous content: a simple time-based trigger releases new material.

An achievement-based rule might have students take an online test at the end of each module. Only those passing the test can access the next module.

Drip-feed systems have their supporters and detractors. Those in favour claim that the slow reveal helps prevent a feeling of overwhelm and allows students to focus on one area of learning at a time. By releasing content in stages, students can work through the course materials at their own pace while still feeling a sense of progression and accomplishment.

Detractors believe students should see the full extent of what's on offer and have the freedom to make up their own minds as to how they engage with the material.

There is no clear right or wrong, however, make sure you have a clear understanding of what your prospective LMS offers.

User management

Your LMS should provide management tools that cover all users, not just students and instructors. Potentially, you may need to manage markers, creators, administrators, mentors, etc. All these people will need differing levels of secure access. You'll want the ability to create and manage user accounts, assign roles, permissions, and access levels, and monitor user activity.

It's clear that this can quickly become a complex topic—you end up having to manage something akin to an online village. Time spent in advance, analyzing the access requirements of your likely users is time well spent.

Reporting and analytics

You'll want reporting that allows administrators to track and analyze student progress, course completion rates, engagement, etc. You might want the LMS to automatically grade assignments. This saves instructor time and gives students instant feedback. Regardless of how assignments are graded, you'll want instructors to be able to monitor student progress, for example, which lessons have been completed, how much time students have spent on each task, and how well they have performed on assessments. This data can be used to identify areas where students are struggling and to provide additional support or resources as needed.

You might also want to track hours spent by instructors and course creators. Student feedback on content and instructors will also need collecting and analyzing.

This chapter considers the internal use of an LMS to support staff training. However, if the system were supporting courses sold to fee-paying clients, you can easily see how a whole new layer of reporting becomes desirable. In this latter case, you'll want to analyze the data in many ways, apart from the obvious revenue by course. For example, you might want to know how quickly students complete courses, their average assessment scores, the range of final scores, or the most popular course according to student feedback. The rabbit burrow can very rapidly become very deep.

Mobile access

Google is very serious about wanting all of us to deliver a top-quality service to all users, regardless of the device they are using. All LMS providers seem to have taken this message to heart and so you can be confident that whatever system you select, it should be mobile friendly. That said, it does no harm to check, and you might also want to ask if the LMS provider provides additional functionality, such as a mobile app, or browser extension.

Communication tools

Some LMS providers build communication channels within their platforms, so students and instructors can communicate without leaving the platform. In some instances, you'll find integrated messaging and discussion forums. I view these as being nice-to-have, rather than mandatory, but know that they exist and assign them a value that suits your needs.

Gamification and social learning

This has been the latest craze to sweep through the LMS market—the ability to integrate elements, such as badges, rewards, and leaderboards, to motivate learners and promote engagement.

So far as I can tell, the jury is still out on whether it improves learning outcomes. (To me, gamification comes across as suppliers looking for ways to differentiate their platforms, more than a serious effort to improve learning outcomes—but that's a personal bias, not based in fact.)

Integrations

This is important: the ability to integrate with other systems and tools, such as ecommerce platforms, payment gateways, CRM systems, content-authoring tools, and virtual classroom platforms. Look at the integrations available and how they are delivered, for example via a *webhook* or an *application processing interface* (API)— see Chapter 2 for a reminder on this. It's worth knowing the subtle differences, as the two integration methods can help make learning a seamless experience for students and instructors, as well as streamline administration and data management.

Accessibility and compliance

All the normal accessibility provisions apply here too. Relevant regulations and standards are Section 508[7] and WCAG[8.] These cover provision of alternative content formats, such as audio descriptions and closed captions, and ensure that the LMS platform is compatible with assistive technologies.

LMS platforms may have distinct features and functionalities depending on their target audience, industry focus, and business model. However, this list is a good starting point.

---

7 Section 508: accessibility requirements for IT systems. See https://section508.gov
8 WCAG: Web Content Accessibility Guidelines. See https://wcag.com/

7.

The Monthly Performance Review

There can be few employees—or managers—who look forward to the ritual of performance reviews. When mentioning website performance stats, I see a similar glazing of the eyes and shuffling of feet; the need to be in some meeting elsewhere. This is understandable, as so much of website performance monitoring seems to lie somewhere on a scale between opaque and dark art. It's time to shine a light into the dark corners and bring some clarity, enabling you to ask your IT colleagues insightful questions.

First, the website performance metrics that directly impact your business. Whatever else you're offered, make sure you've got a handle on the following. Later, I follow up with an introduction to tools useful to non-IT professionals. Your IT department may not give you free choice over performance tools. However, it's helpful to know what's available in case you can influence purchasing decisions.

Load Speed

Nobody likes to be kept waiting. Customers appreciate fast service in a physical store, and equally, they expect your website to load quickly. A fast-loading website improves user experience, reduces bounce rates, and increases the likelihood of visitors converting into customers. Google formally recognized load speed as a 'mid-ranking' factor as part of its Core Web Vitals update, announced in 2021. By February 2022, the rollout was complete to all sites, mobile and desktop.

Some people may tell you that load speed isn't that important, as—from Google's perspective—it's only a mid-ranking factor. Don't be seduced by this argument. Google has long stated their belief that load speed is important. Expect increased focus on this, not less.

This isn't an academic treatise, so I'll not bore you with the details from many studies. Be assured that firms such as Amazon, Walmart, and Akamai have done a lot of testing, and all are in broad agreement with Google's finding: speed matters.

Mobile Devices & Responsiveness

There are nearly 7 billion smartphones out there, meaning that 86% of the world's population owns such a device.[9] Add in tablets and laptops, and the total mobile population is huge. So, you'd expect firms to be constantly keeping on top of their website's *mobile* performance. And yet...

If your department delivers information via your company's website, then you can guarantee it will be viewed on a mobile device. Do yourself, and your colleagues, a huge favour: make sure the website performance reports sent your way clearly break out mobile versus desktop performance. Don't let yourself be fobbed off with some non-specific, generic average.

9   Statista 2023: 6.92 billion smartphones worldwide.

User Engagement

Business websites exist to generate sales or leads, so it's vital to monitor how users interact with your website. How long are they staying on your site? What pages are they visiting? Are they clicking on important links?

When performance metrics were developed, the focus was on individual website pages (or content), as opposed to the visitor's journey through the site. This latter concept of a *visitor journey* is relatively new and undergoing rapid change. There are several exciting tools available (more on them later).

Conversion Rates

A natural follow-on from monitoring how visitors *engage* with your website, is measuring how many *convert* (into either customers or leads). Conversions are the 'ultimate' metric and one of the first to be tracked. For this reason, conversion tracking is well developed and all ecommerce systems, email systems and sign-up forms have good conversion-tracking capabilities, so you can insist on detailed reports—your IT colleagues have the data available.

SEO Performance

Search Engine Optimization (SEO) is crucial for driving organic traffic to your website. Monitor your website's SEO performance by tracking your keyword rankings, organic traffic, and backlinks. Improving your SEO can increase your website's visibility in search engine results, making it easier for potential customers to find you online.

SEO can seem overwhelming to many non-IT professionals. This is understandable, as much of the confusion lies with the label "search engine optimization". Not only is it unhelpful, it's plain wrong! Here's why.

Suppose an architect offered an "office layout optimization" service. You'd reasonably assume the service *optimized office layouts*. Your local car dealership might advertise "car engine tuning" and it's clear what the service does.

This familiar, linguistic logic breaks down when applied to the term *search engine optimization*. It's not the search engine that's being optimized, but your website. SEO should more correctly be called "website optimization" and I can't help but feel that if it was, there would be a lot less confusion among non-technically qualified personnel. That said, I know I'm a lonely salmon swimming against a very strong current, so you and I are just going to have to live with the misleading "SEO" label.

Whatever it's called, SEO plays a vital role in improving your website's visibility and organic web traffic (from search engines like Google). Business professionals can usefully contribute to three major areas of SEO activity—here's a summary of each.

Keyword research

The identification of the specific words (or phrases) used by people when searching for products or services related to your business. Understanding these keywords can help you align your website's content to the needs of your target audience.

On-page optimization

This is the term used to collectively label many topics, each of which has some impact on page content and the visibility of the page in search results. For example, page titles, meta descriptions, headers, how keywords are incorporated. Also included is the optimization of your overall website—its hierarchy, structure, and internal links.

Backlink building

Backlinks are links from other websites pointing to your site. Search engines interpret backlinks as a vote of confidence. However, similar to votes of confidence in the human world, not all votes count equally. Your best friend passing on the exceptional service they received at a local restaurant is probably worth more to you than a comment from a stranger you meet on the train. Backlinks are given a numerical rank and the bigger the number, the better the link. A link from a trusted source, such as the BBC or CNN will be worth more than a link from Joe's General Store.

Building high-quality backlinks from reputable websites is an important part of your overall SEO strategy. A detail that's worth your attention is the *anchor text*. This is the text the reader clicks on (to trigger the backlink). For example, the backlink might be to this page on your site:

https://website-domain.com/amazing-product

Suppose a website offered you a choice between the following backlink texts. Which would you pick (all other things being equal)?

"...**click here** to find out more about reducing your energy bills..."

"...find out how to **reduce your energy bills** and maintain a..."

In both cases, the clickable text (underlined) is the anchor text and both examples lead to the same URL. In the first example, the clickable text is a generic phrase. In the second example, the clickable text is a keyword phrase. The second is more valuable to you than the first. However, if used too frequently, Google will suspect you might have unreasonable influence over the backlink text (and may demote the value of the link). Most of your backlink anchor texts should simply be your company name or domain, or the URL of a specific page on your site. Occasionally, use customized text if you're offered the opportunity.

Security

Protecting customer data is an essential aspect of maintaining trust. Your IT colleagues should monitor the wider aspects of your website's security measures (such as SSL certificates, firewall protection, software updates, etc.).

You have a responsibility at a departmental level to ensure careless mistakes don't cause bigger problems. The most common issues are passwords on open display and screens unlocked while the user is away from their desk. (I have a friend whose business is IT security. He's also a keen amateur photographer. He showed me a series of photographs he'd taken from a seventh floor hotel balcony, facing the office block across the street. Using a telephoto lens, he captured completely legible images of several computer monitors, from unoccupied desks. Something as simple as a screensaver would have thwarted his snooping.)

Website Traffic Meets Visitor Journeys

Monitoring website performance is as old as websites themselves. Having some historical context will help you understand the fractured, messy market of website performance monitoring. Rudimentary website traffic measurement tools appeared in the mid-1990s and the market developed rapidly. Approximately a decade later, in-depth optimization tools made their first appearance.

In 2005 Google introduced Analytics and turned the website traffic analysis market on its head. Many users—technical and non-technical—struggled with the different tools and metrics. However, there was one big difference between Google Analytics and all the other tools: Google Analytics was free. This simple fact unhinged the market and led directly to Analytics becoming the dominant tool for measuring website traffic. (From a user perspective, this was great news, but I still feel for those software companies wiped out by Google's ploy: it's hard to compete against a company with deep wallets giving away a good product for free.)

Fast-forward another decade or so (to around 2015) and there's a renaissance in website performance monitoring. The new kid on the block being *visitor journeys*—distinct and different from *website traffic*. Marketers took control of tool design, and tools that were directly helpful in making business decisions entered the market.

That's twenty years of software development in three paragraphs, so forgive me for skipping a few details: you get the general idea. Now that you're up to speed, here's what's under the covers.

Google Analytics

Google Analytics is a powerful and complex product. For getting insight into many high-level marketing issues, many marketers view Analytics as a sledgehammer to crack a nut. (Certainly, in the SME marketplace, its complexity overwhelms many website owners.) While it's great to know you can call on in-depth analysis, it's more than what's needed to support most business decisions. Your IT colleagues will use Google Analytics and Google Search Console to supply you with useful information, but you don't need to spend so much time with it. My objective is to help you work with specialists to get the needs of your business met, not to convert you into an expert user of traffic-analysis tools.

Google Analytics reports two headline metrics that are both useful and easy to access: *pageviews* and *visitor sessions*:

Pageviews tells you the number of times a page has been seen—including multiple views by the same visitor.

A *visitor session* measures the time a visitor is on your site. Sessions can include several pageviews.

You might also come across *unique pageviews*. This measures the number of pageviews generated by a single visitor during a single session.

In summary, unique pageviews tells you how many visitors have viewed a particular page, while pageviews is the total number of times your site displayed a page.

There is much more to Google Analytics than pageviews and sessions. If you want to measure an event that's important to your business (for example, a visitor completing a form or watching a video), you'll want to research *conversion events*. A simple internet search will tell you all you need to know.

Tracking Visitor Journeys and Behaviour

As mentioned, the concept of visitor journeys (and our ability to track them) is newer than our ability to track pageviews and sessions. Tracking visitor journeys has huge business value, so you should know more about it and how it's done.

Imagine you have connected a tool like Google Analytics to a piano keyboard (stick with me—this exercise will make sense). The tool could tell you many intricate details. For example, when the pianist struck each key, whether the note was in tune, the pressure exerted on the keys, the duration each key was depressed, the pedal positions associated with each key depression, etc. You get the picture—lots of highly detailed information that would be useful, if you were a music instrument designer wanting to build a better piano, or you were tuning the piano for a special rendition.

But what if you're not a music instrument designer and don't need all this detail? What if you simply want to know who's playing the piano and what tune they are playing? This is like a visitor journey. Who approached the piano? Did they just look at it, or did they sit down and play a tune? How long were they playing? How many tunes did they play, and what were they?

The difference? The first set of data is all about the mechanics of the piano. The second set is all about who is using the piano and how they are interacting with it. You need tools that can provide you with both sets of data.

Getting back to your website, here are four key questions regarding website traffic and content:

- Are visitors seeing the important content?

- Are they clicking where we want them to (on key page sections)?

- To what degree are they distracted?

- Is any non-clickable content causing confusion?

These questions are all concerned with the behaviour of visitors during their journeys through your website.

Figure 7-1 illustrates a typical user journey, to help you visualize how journeys and behaviours differ from pageviews and sessions.

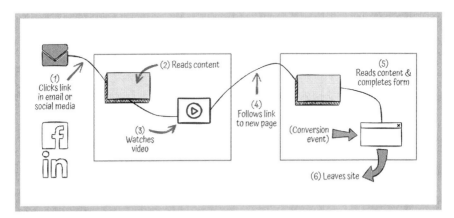

Figure 7-1: Visitor journeys and behaviour analysis focus on how visitors move through and interact with a website.

Step 1: Intrigued by what they read, the visitor clicks on a link in an email and is taken to a website page.

Step 2: Arriving at the page, they read the content.

Step 3. Wanting to know more, they watch the video (on the same page).

Step 4. Having watched the video, they click another link and are taken to another page, where...

Step 5. ...they read more content, including a call-to-action, that leads them to complete a form.

Step 6. The visitor clicks the 'submit' button on the form and leaves the site.

The visitor's journey has spanned two webpages, two blocks of copy, a video, and ended with them completing a form. You can easily appreciate the value of this 'joined-up' view, versus how the same metrics might appear if represented in a spreadsheet, in a disconnected manner. I know your next question: you want to know what tools are available to help you track visitor journeys. Read on.

Visitor Tracking and Behaviour Analysis Tools

All the tools introduced in this section were announced between 2014 and 2020. That's a good chunk of time after Google's initial release of Analytics in 2005. Visitor journey and behaviour analysis is a rapidly developing market and so I'm going to focus on approaches and outcomes, skipping transient technical details. All the tools reviewed offer something slightly different and used together with Google's tools will give you a comprehensive view of your website visitors.

Funnelytics

Canadian entrepreneur and marketeer Mikael Dia launched Funnelytics in 2018, partly through his own frustration with deriving valuable marketing material from existing tools, such as Google Analytics.

In a brief space of time the Funnelytics team developed a remarkable tool that adopts an intuitive and novel two-step approach.

The first step recognizes our natural desire for wanting to draw the layout of a website. Used in this mode, Funnelytics performs like a specialized drawing package, akin to a mashup between Miro, PowerPoint, and AutoCAD, for example.

The second step reveals the tool's superpower. With just a few keystrokes you're able to make the drawing of your website 'live' by connecting it to the internet and watching how traffic moves through all the pages of your site. Imagine a 'live' version of Figure 7-1 and you won't be far off the mark.

Funnelytics is a beautiful tool for showing businesspeople how their website is being used. It's easy to see how visitors arrive, the popular pages they visit, where they go to next and finally, where they exit the site.

In summary, Funnelytics allows you to:

- Sketch a website plan, showing all the pages and connections between them. It could be an existing site, or one you plan on creating.

- For existing sites, you can connect real page URLs to the layout and see how traffic flows through the site.

- You can go further and show more details, such as scroll depth and button clicks on individual pages.

I'm happy to declare an interest, as I was an early investor in Funnelytics. We use the tool at Active Presence to underpin some of our services.

https://funnelytics.io

Hotjar

Hotjar's aim is to help you keep people on your website for as long as possible. For example, it can detect parts of your site that aren't attracting attention, so you can redesign or remove them.

Hotjar's heatmaps locate the most activity on each webpage. You can quickly discover the parts of your site visitors find interesting and the areas they skip over. For example, suppose your website lists services by category. If the Categories tab is getting lots of attention, you can reasonably presume visitors want to view your content according to your predefined categories. Another example could be scroll depth. If you see a lot of visitors scrolling all the way to the page footer, it might suggest they aren't finding what they are looking for. (Highly engaged visitors might also scroll the full length of the page, but will most likely remain on the page longer, so you have to make a judgment based on overall visitor behaviour.)

You can access different Hotjar heatmaps. The *click-heatmap* illustrates where visitors click (and their click frequency). The *move-heatmap* shows you where visitors are hovering their mouse. The *scroll-heatmap* gives you the percentage of a page viewed.

https://hotjar.com

Microsoft Clarity

Clarity and Hotjat are similar tools. Microsoft announced Clarity in 2018, with full public access from the end of October 2020. As Hotjar launched in 2014, Microsoft is the new kid on the block and their approach to pricing Clarity makes it worthy of mention.

Hotjar offers a free restricted-function licence, with the tool's full capabilities being accessible via a monthly subscription. In stark contrast, Microsoft announced Clarity as 'free forever'. (Remember Google's announcement of Analytics, back in 2005?)

Clarity offers heatmaps, session recordings, and connection with Google Analytics. Some Hotjar supporters claim that Clarity isn't as comprehensive, but Clarity is the newer tool. At the time of writing (3Q23) Hotjar's free forever plan includes automatic data capture, unlimited heatmaps, and HubSpot integration. If you have little experience with heatmaps and tracking user interaction, dipping your toe into the water with a free tool would seem to make a lot of sense, and for that you could use Clarity or Hotjar's free plan.

Some other tools similar to Clarity and Hotjar include; Crazy Egg, MouseFlow, Inspectlet, Smartlook, and HeatMap.

https://clarity.microsoft.com

You now have a good feeling for how a website can contribute to various aspects of your business. You understand the key issues that ought to be agreed between business departments and your colleagues in IT. You have some 'sanity check' checklists and enough knowledge of some technical vocabulary not to feel intimidated.

What else can you do to ensure a smooth working relationship with IT bods, when you find yourself seconded to your organization's next website project? Part C has the answers.

Part C

Working With
IT Folk

8.

The Who's Who of IT

Increasing complexity makes teamwork essential for IT projects, as no one person can do it all. Understanding how a business captures and manipulates data, and then converts the outcome into an integrated set of triggers and messages is a complex undertaking.

Here's an introduction to the roles typically needed in modern website projects. Not all these roles are needed all the time, but all are needed some of the time.

Marketing Strategist

This role is incredibly valuable for non-IT staff. If you have these people on board, become their newfound best friend as soon as possible. The marketing strategist sits at the interface of marketing and IT and sets expectations for the business and the IT team.

I've come across many owners of small businesses who mistakenly believe they can do this themselves. While it's tempting to believe that nobody could know more than you about what you do or the market you serve, this misses two important points:

1. The marketing strategist will have experience of other IT and web-design projects. This helps them create realistic deadlines and track progress. In this context, they're bringing project management skills to the party.

2. They act as a decision maker and communications channel. They know the decisions they can take to keep a project on track, and when to escalate issues outside the project team.

Business Analyst

The role of the business analyst (BA) is as old as IT itself, so it's worth knowing what they do. Business analysts are experts in understanding what a business does with the data it has. It's easy to appreciate how a business analyst is going to be way more important to international banking than to the corner grocery store. That said, many smaller businesses are venturing into ecommerce, which automatically produces more complex data flows.

You should also make friends with business analysts. They will want to know the end-user story inside out, back to front, and upside down. And, as the Business Representative, they'll expect you to know it too. They can smell a rat at fifty paces and will expose any processes that are poorly documented or comments such as, "We've always done it this way". Their dedication is well intentioned. All the work done by developers and designers relies on the BA's output. Help them do a great job and your project will stand a much greater chance of completing on time and within budget.

Smaller companies (and smaller projects) sometimes try to get away without having a business analyst on the team. If you find yourself in that position, ask how the BA role will be covered. Keep asking until you get an answer you can live with.

Systems Architect

When I joined the nascent IT sector in my early twenties, the role of 'architect' didn't exist[10]. The internet triggered a rapid expansion of new technologies, platforms, programming languages, etc. As projects became more complex, both in scope and the number of subsystems, a need arose for someone to define the various technology components projects would use. That person is the systems architect: the person who recommends what IT components should be used to achieve the project's business goals.

As with business analysts, smaller businesses won't have enough work to need a dedicated systems architect. However, appreciating the role can help you understand how key IT systems decisions *ought to be* made. I stress *ought to be*, as I've come across projects in which important decisions were made by default and for the wrong reason. For example, I recall an ecommerce project that used the Shopify ecommerce platform. (To be clear, there's nothing inherently wrong with that. I view Shopify as a great platform.) Digging deeper, it emerged that the decision to use Shopify was driven by the ecommerce specialist—and he recommended it simply because it was the platform he was most comfortable using. Might there have been another platform that better suited the needs of the business? Who knows? The question was never asked.

Systems architecture decisions have long-lasting consequences. Once you're committed to a particular ecommerce system, for example, changing it is complex and expensive. Take the time you need to feel comfortable with the people advising you at this level. Do they have long IT careers? Have they worked on diverse projects, preferably in the same sector for similarly sized businesses?

10 The IT sector's attempt to use the word 'architect' caused a bit of a faff, especially in the UK, where the title 'architect' is a professionally protected term. Eventually the title 'systems architect' was accepted by all involved.

Designer (of various sorts)

As the IT sector has matured, the term 'designer' has developed. It's a much-misused label, so it's worthwhile clarifying its various uses.

Graphic designers are specialists at using images to communicate concepts. They know about fonts, colours, layout, typography, etc. For many, the bedrock of their early career was advertising (especially print advertising if they are an older designer). You'll also find that many have worked in marketing, communications, or branding.

Website designer is an informal label that has arisen through common usage. The arrival of high-quality content management systems (Squarespace, for example) gave graphic designers new openings—they could now create good-looking websites for grateful clients. Although this market has been successful for many years, cracks are appearing in the plaster. The advertising background of many graphic designers leaves them ill-equipped to deal with modern, complex projects, as they lack the necessary technical skills.

As websites increased in complexity, it made sense to break down design into more specialist areas. The Wikipedia entry for 'web design' is a useful starting point. It refers to 'web design' as the *"...many different skills and disciplines in the production and maintenance of websites..."* The same article talks about graphic design, *user interface (UI) design*, and *user experience (UX) design*. Within IT, these terms are well understood and used in preference to the general label of 'website designer'.

Outside the IT bubble, clients and suppliers alike use the term 'web designer' as a catchall term for several distinct functions within IT and website development. Here's an introduction to UI and UX design.

- **UI design** focuses on system aesthetics. UI design is highly visual. For example, can users easily find the information they're looking for? Do they intuitively know what action to take?

- **UX design** focuses on how well a system works. UX designers concentrate on removing friction. They want to create a system that makes it easy for the user to achieve what the business owner wants. UX designers are skilled in research, testing, and validating alternative designs. (For this reason, some UX designers prefer the label UX specialist, as opposed to designer.)

So, if someone describes themselves as a 'website designer', what exactly do they do? Good question. Nowadays, anyone with good UI or UX credentials would call them out loud and proud. If someone describes themselves as a 'website designer', I'd interpret that as a *'Jack or Jill of all trades'*, with potentially greater strength in the visual (graphic design) side of website design. If they had strong IT skills, then they would be more likely to call themselves a website developer (see next).

In summary, the term 'website designer' is a bit of a mess, especially at the smaller end of the market.

Website Developer

Website developers work with code. They use programming languages and other technologies to make a website function as required by the design specification. They're not concerned with what it looks like, they're concerned with what it does. They work closely with UX specialists.

Other Specialist Roles

Beyond the foundation work, there are various specialists who can help improve websites. Their roles are more self-explanatory and easier to grasp.

The objective of Search Engine Optimization is to help your target audience discover your website. The *SEO specialist* improves your website's organic search engine ranking. They research the search terms used by your ideal clients and focus your website on responding with high-quality content. They might also edit your site layout, so it is looked on more favourably by search engines. The goal is to have your website appear on the first page of search results. Over two thirds of all clicks go to the first five organic results[11] and fewer than 1% of Google searchers bother with results on the second page[12]. SEO used to be something that website owners could do themselves. However, the growth in the number of sites and their complexity has made SEO an expert domain, even though some basic concepts have remained (such as the value of backlinks).

The natural companion to organic traffic is traffic you pay for (via advertising of some form). Pay per click (PPC) advertising is the most common form, in which you only pay when users click on your advert (and get directed to your website). Advertising is a complex area. A lot of testing and tuning is required to get adverts performing well, i.e. attracting traffic that converts well for a reasonable outlay. There are many variables and *PPC Specialists* are the people who can help you.

The major PPC platforms (e.g. Facebook, LinkedIn, Google, Amazon) have their own business objectives, none of which involve being parsimonious with your advertising budget. If you show them

---

11   https://www.zerolimitweb.com/organic-vs-ppc-2021-ctr-results-best-practices/
12   https://backlinko.com/google-ctr-stats

your bank account, they'll delight in emptying it. PPC advertising works by running an auction between advertisers wanting to bid for the same advertising slot. The winner isn't necessarily the person who bids the most, but the person whose advert is most likely to succeed. Specialists will help tune your adverts, so you can get more clicks for fewer dollars.

The job of the PPC specialist is to use your budget wisely to generate high volumes of the right traffic and deliver it to where you tell them. If they do that, and the traffic fails to convert, that could be the fault of where the traffic lands and not of the advertising. There's little point in a PPC specialist working hard to produce perfect leads if those leads end up on a home page full of non-specific, wishy-washy copy. PPC works best when it's used to generate traffic for a highly specific niche offer. The page at which that traffic arrives should focus on the needs of the PPC-generated audience.

Ecommerce is another area that has developed rapidly and now benefits from specialist attention. Ecommerce is similar to SEO and PPC, in that the early shopping carts were relatively simple affairs that could be configured by competent designers. Nowadays, *Ecommerce Specialists* work with systems (such as Shopify) that are so rich in function they can replace an entire website, as opposed to being an adjunct to an existing one. In the WordPress world you can find dedicated ecommerce plugins (such as WooCommerce) and there are plenty of WordPress experts who make a good living just focusing their efforts on WooCommerce, and leaving the 'ordinary website setup' to others.

Copywriters

Copywriters are the unsung champions that underpin all successful websites, funnels, and landing pages. Writing for the web differs from writing offline documents, in that there is less space available to get the job done. Successful online copy is direct and efficient. It uses specific techniques to capture and hold attention, and lead towards an outcome. Good copywriters are worth their weight in gold, so make sure there's one on your team.

9.

Tips for Happy
IT Projects

In my forty-plus years of working in IT, I've witnessed many successful projects. I've also witnessed some projects that went completely off the rails. Early in my career—and too naïve to disaster-dodge—I ended up in the middle of two calamitous projects. Although neither was of my making, I found myself 'volunteered' as part of the clean-up crew: fresh faces, parachuted in to put things right. I was young, lacking experience and way out of my depth. Those painful times taught me huge amounts and led to me being offered some plum opportunities later in life. This chapter is a mixture of the wisdom that comes with grey hair, along with the commonly understood way of 'getting things done'. Both are complementary, neither being at odds with the other. In what follows, I call out the grey wisdom from the black-and-white of the textbook, so you have a clear idea as to my experience versus the formal approach of the IT profession.

There are many cases of interdisciplinary teams in all walks of life. The borders between the disciplines frequently causes stress, confusion, and disagreement. What happens when you put IT and non-IT folk together? It's time to find out.

Differences Between IT and Non-IT Projects

It's useful to highlight several major differences between IT projects and general business-oriented projects:

Technical complexity

IT projects are technically complex and, in that sense, more akin to complex engineering projects. IT projects require many specialists, each with different and complementary knowledge and expertise (e.g. UX and UI design, coding, database design). Managing the deployment of these skills is a large part of the Project Manager's job (as highly specialized staff are very expensive). While general business-oriented projects may involve some specialist skills, they tend to focus more on business operations or processes.

Project scope (and change management)

IT projects run to a tightly defined scope. The scope is the first thing an IT Project Manager will check (and, if they're a subcontractor, they'll most likely decline a project they consider to be poorly scoped). IT projects are expensive and a poorly scoped project risks running out of budget before it achieves its objectives.

Of course, the world doesn't stand still. We all know requirements change. Well-managed IT projects have a clear change management process and change budget to help bridge the gap between a fixed, tight scope and the shifting sands of reality. The Project Manager will insist all scope changes go through the change management process.

An important note regarding the 'change budget'. Many non-IT professionals reasonably assume the change budget to be money set aside to pay for any scope changes during the project's life. Wrong. IT staff are expensive, and so *all* their time has to be accounted for. The change budget covers the calculation of how much the change would cost if it were to proceed. So, the change budget is *not* used to pay for changes, just for working out how much a change would cost.

To non-IT folk this might sound a bit crazy, but it's born of experience, and with good intent. For example, an innocent sounding request, such as, "Can we have a purple button, instead of a blue lever?" could have unforeseen consequences. The "blue lever" might have already gone through unit testing and integration testing. Changing it to a "purple button" means doing all those tests again, leading to increased cost and time delays.

The change budget is used to work out the likely impact of implementing the "purple button". This allows the Project Manager and Business Representative—that's you, by the way—to have a meaningful conversation.

Project Manager, "The original spec called for a blue lever and as the blue lever has successfully passed integration testing, we're reasonably confident that the system test will go without a hitch. Building a purple button isn't, of itself, that expensive, but its introduction at this late stage would trigger a lot of retesting. This will most likely increase the project cost by £50,000 and lead to a six week delay. Can the business live with that?"

The contribution of the change budget was to pay for the calculation of the two figures: £50k cost increase and six-week delay. Armed with this knowledge, the project owners (most likely the business department) can decide whether they really do want their "purple button" after all. All changes cost money and time, it's simply a question of degree.

Project timeline

IT projects have complex timelines, broken into mini projects (commonly referred to within IT as 'sprints'). This makes IT projects susceptible to even quite minor delays. If you find yourself seconded to an IT project, make friends with the Project Manager early on, and do your best to understand where likely pinch points might be. You'll inevitably be gathering input from business colleagues who aren't formally associated with the project. It's up to you to ensure the business delivers their input in sync with the overall plan.

Stakeholder involvement

IT gets its tentacles into every part of the business, so it follows that IT projects frequently have more stakeholders than many general business-oriented projects.

Managing multiple stakeholders can be challenging. Typically, the IT project will be just one of many plates they are trying to keep spinning. Getting stakeholder attention when the project needs it is frequently a drain on the project manager's time.

Risk management

The sheer number of moving parts within IT projects makes them riskier than many. Add to that, technical complexity, tight timelines, and multiple stakeholders, and you have the perfect project manager's nightmare.

Deliverables

IT projects typically deliver tangible results, such as a new order management system, a new website, or a new online booking system. Many business projects focus on incremental improvement of the status quo, for example, improving expense management, or implementing organizational changes.

Non-IT Staff on IT Projects

Imagine you're seconded to a team whose job is delivering a new website for your company. Reasonably enough, the business holds the IT department responsible for the project, and a team leader is appointed from within the IT ranks. Your role is to represent the interests of the business, ensuring that the business objectives are met. What could you do to help the team deliver the website the business needs?

Articulate business goals

As far as the team is concerned, you own the business goals, so you'd better be clear about them.

> **Grey Wisdom Moment**
>
> The failure of many projects can be traced back to inadequate understanding of the goals. Business analysts and marketing strategists are your allies in making sure the team understands what they need to deliver to satisfy your colleagues in the business.

You are the 'voice of the user', so make sure you understand what the users want and that you can articulate this with crystal clear clarity. This will help your IT colleagues understand what functionality and features are needed and set a priority for each.

Provide user feedback

You're the conduit for user feedback regarding usability, design, and overall look and feel. Make sure you have a handle on what types of content and functionality the intended users find most valuable.

> **Grey Wisdom Moment**
>
> Modern IT projects progress via a series of tightly defined development sprints. It's important that input is delivered in a timely way before the start of each sprint. This means you'll request feedback on multiple occasions, from people whose day job, most likely, does not include giving your project the feedback it needs. They think they're 'doing you a favour' and you're at the bottom of their to-do list. The reality is that their role is critical, and you need their input on time.

Collaborate with the IT professionals

It sounds obvious, but sometimes the obvious needs to be expressly stated: turn up for more than just the required project meetings. Given that you're reading this book, you'll understand the importance of this, so I won't bang on about it. Suffice to say, most IT departments are one step removed from the sharp edge of the business, i.e. the profit-generating departments, which win all the accolades at company away days.

I'm about to state some sweeping generalizations, so they won't be universally true. However, I hope you see them as being true enough to support the point I want to make.

IT departments tend to have the youngest staff. If the company has recruited well, they'll be technically well qualified, as well as bright-eyed and bushy-tailed. With youthfulness comes inexperience. Young IT professionals may know their IT, but they frequently lack the life experience to deal with the nuances of everyday business life. You have bucketloads of business experience. In their eyes, that's a huge thing you can bring to the party. Be proud of what your department does, how it does it, and the contribution it makes. From my own days as a young systems engineer, it felt great working on projects that delivered real business benefit.

The key is to explain to the IT department how important the project is to the business. That value might seem obvious to you, but it may not be to your colleagues in IT. They're not in the business, they're *supporting* it: big difference.

Demonstrate a willingness to understand the technical feasibility of different ideas and approaches. Ask IT staff to outline their development process and technical requirements, so you can help them achieve their objectives.

Prioritize features and functionality

The above emphasis on the difference between being in the business, as opposed to supporting it, also applies here. You know the business needs and you represent the users. Your input regarding features and functionality is vital to the project's success.

Be as clear as you can, as your IT colleagues may see cheaper or quicker ways of delivering what you want via an alternative technology. Here's a quick story to illustrate the point about being clear.

The origin of this story lies in the computerization of the Wimbledon Tennis Championships in the late 1980s. In one of the many committee meetings at the All England Club, one of most respected and experienced officials said,

"All we need to know is when the ball's in and when it's out."

A young 28-year-old IT geek (that'll be me) begged to differ.

"I'm not sure that's true, is it?" I said. "We could design a system to do that, but I think all you really need to know is when the ball is out. Surely you don't also need to know when it's in."

The silence was palpable and long. Even the church mouse held its breath. Finally, a delightful fellow official, with whom I'd been working closely, came to my rescue,

"He's right—I know the way he speaks."

Order restored, feathers unruffled, the meeting continued. (As I type, IBM continues as the official IT supplier to The Championships and the All England Club. An association that started at the 1990 Championships.)

You see the point the young 28-year-old me was making? What if we'd just pressed ahead and produced a system that did way more than was necessary, by signaling whether *every* ball was either in or out? Shown such a system, I'm sure the officials would have said, "But we don't need to know when the ball is in. Why did you build it like that?"

Be precise. Be prepared for close and detailed questioning. As my dear departed Dad frequently reminded me, "Time spent in reconnaissance is seldom wasted."

Non-IT Staff and Testing

Testing is a huge topic, and an IT profession in its own right. You ought to be directly involved in *some* aspects of testing. Having a wider understanding will help you ensure the project delivers business goals and objectives. Here are some testing stages you should know about:

Unit testing

This is an early stage of testing. Individual components or modules of the website are tested to ensure they are working as expected. Imagine a selection of children's building blocks scattered over a carpet. The test is focused on the efficacy of a subset of the blocks.

Sometimes, non-IT professionals are dismissive of unit testing, "I'll wait until there's more to comment on before saying anything." Please resist this temptation. Every test is an important milestone, regardless of how minor it might appear to you.

Integration testing

This is the stage where different modules or components of the website are combined and tested together to ensure that they are working as a whole. Following the above building-block analogy, several blocks have now been united to build three walls of a building. Is this what you expected? Are the door frames and window frames in the right place, etc?

System testing

The website is deemed as complete and is tested as a complete system. Does it meet the functional specification and business objectives? All the building blocks have been combined and there is a magnificent medieval castle in the middle of the lounge carpet. Is it complete and medieval enough?

Acceptance testing

This is the final stage of testing where the website meets (business) reality. Sometimes, you might see it referred to as the CAT (Customer Acceptance Test). However named, it refers to the system being tested against real-world scenarios. Feedback from real users ensures it meets user requirements and the needs of the business. As for the medieval castle sitting proudly on the lounge carpet, little Jimmy's frustration that the moat can't be filled with real water is a great example of how setting clear user expectations early on can help avoid later disappointment.

Well-managed IT projects have many testing milestones. You don't need to know about all of them, but knowing about the above four will help you keep the project on track from a business perspective.

Testing is an iterative process. Bugs or useability issues might arise during a system test, even though they didn't during unit or integration testing. This is the nature of software development and that's why well-managed testing is critical to ensuring the website meets the needs of the business.

That's it. You made it. I set out to write a short guide because I know you're not super interested in IT for the sake of it. You want to know enough to do your job better. As far as websites are concerned, that's what I've given you. You're now a website wrangler looking for the next project. Having made this investment in yourself, keep it going by joining the online Website Wisdom Community. You can meet others like yourself and keep up to speed (and it doesn't cost you a bean).

https://WebsiteWisdom.co.uk

Coming up, you'll find some additional notes from me and the first few pages of the next book in the *Website Wisdom Collection*— it's all about website optimization for small businesses.

If you're leaving now, I'd be grateful if you would post a review on the site where you bought this book. Books need reviews, as engines need fuel. Without them, they simply can't do the work they have to do.

Author's Note & Acknowledgements

I'm delighted you're reading this sentence. As it's toward the end of the book, there's a fair chance you will also have read many of the earlier sentences that give meaning to the 27,000 words between the covers.

Books are read the same way they're written: sentence by sentence. Each is unique. It has a job to do, and once done, can rest until called upon again.

Even though the transfer of knowledge via books is as old as the hills, it remains a fascinating and somewhat risky process. You and I know a limited amount about one another, and outside of these pages may never meet (which is a sad thought—more later). Based on this limited knowledge, I've had to construct a conversation between us, in which I imagined your side of the discussion and gave you the perfect response at just the right moment.

How did I do? I'd genuinely like to know. You can reach me via my website:

https://chrisdavidson.co.uk

The recent COVID-19 pandemic shook up many organizations. One of the results was a change in employment status for many people (whether enforced or voluntary). Lots of people were left scrambling around for a new way to make a living, or to secure their existing position. The pandemic also taught us that technology is everywhere in companies nowadays. Business leaders need the knowledge to engage in technical conversations and contribute to decision-making processes. Statements such as, "Oh, that's all down to IT" simply don't cut the mustard any longer.

I wrote *Websites for Business Managers* to give non-IT managers a leg-up in the post-COVID landscape—a landscape characterized by many rapid changes in technology and working patterns. Most of them would have happened this decade anyway, but the pandemic compressed the timescale and triggered mayhem.

Good books don't happen by accident. I could apply all the effort I could muster and use all my innate and learned skills, and still fall short. Ensuring that I didn't are many wonderful people whom I need to thank.

Working from the outside in, my thanks to Scott Graham for his wonderful cover. Scott is a pleasure to work with. He's a hugely creative chap and I could have gone with any of his initial concepts, making the final choice a tough one.

Moving to the inside, I'm grateful to Paula Marais for her diligent editing. Megan Sheer designed what you see between the covers (both print and ebook). Megan's a delight to work with and her beautiful design makes a complex topic easy to follow.

Rob Fitzpatick runs a delightful authors' community, and it's been a pleasure to work with Rob's team and the larger community, sharing the trials and tribulations of getting the job done.

Pacing me on the final sprint to the finish line was Katrina Nichols, who provided first class proofreading. Both Paula and Katrina did sterling work in judging and guiding the mid-Atlantic house style I adopted—a mixture of traditional British and American spellings. Please let me know of any remaining errors, for they certainly belong on my desk and nowhere else.

Thank you also to the Active Presence team, Felix, Elmer, and Mark. They do great work looking after our clients and our own

Author's Note & Acknowledgements

websites. I'm grateful to my mastermind buddies, Niels Brabandt and Paul ter Wal for allowing me to overuse their brains on so many occasions. Lee Warren is a good colleague and professional pal who deserves a mention in despatches. His detailed, polite and professional questioning led to great improvements in the book's title and subtitle. Thank you Lee.

Finally, my thanks to Carol, for helping me navigate the shoals and uncertain channels associated with applying creativity and common sense to an endeavour infamous for its logic and techno-slang.

Whatever the formal agenda of your next business meeting, remember Peter Drucker:

The purpose of a business is to create and keep a customer.

The Website Wisdom Collection and Community

The Collection is published by Active Presence and currently comprises three titles:

Why Your Website Doesn't Work – How to get your message right, focus your website and stop losing business

Published: February 2023

This book is for the owners of service-oriented businesses in the SME (small-to-medium sized enterprises) sector. The book is a complete website improvement toolkit. It includes an online assessment and content management tool (available via download).

Websites for Business Managers – How to Confidently Work with IT Staff, Decode Geek-Speak, and Create the Website Your Business Needs

Published: November 2023

You know all about this book, so no more to add.

Lazy Websites Fixed in Five – 5 Ironclad Steps to SEO Success for Business Owners Frustrated by Impenetrable Geek-Speak

Published: 2024

Optimizing websites for search engine performance has always been a challenge for small businesses. This challenge has become greater in recent years and the necessity to overcome it has become more urgent. This book will fix that problem.

The Website Wisdom Community helps business owners and leaders of small businesses create and manage more effective websites. Visit the website for information about the Collection and Community.

https://websitewisdom.co.uk

Lazy Websites Fixed in Five

5 Ironclad Steps to SEO Success
for Business Owners Frustrated
by Impenetrable Geek-Speak

A PREVIEW OF THE NEXT BOOK IN THE
WEBSITE WISDOM COLLECTION

Optimization is Naturally Part of Your Life

Imagine you live in the small, historic market town of Seonsville in southwest France (population five and a half thousand). The population is proud of the old historic market that dominates the town centre. The central square is pedestrianized during the weekend, when traders come to town and set up their stalls. It's fine weather and you decide to cycle into town. You meet your neighbour, Robert, who is busy building his new bicycle in his driveway. He claims he'll be finished soon and will catch up with you in town later.

Your route takes you past the local car showroom and garage on the edge of town. You notice fresh signs advertising 'car engine tuning' and 'hybrid power train optimization'. The original owner has recently retired and passed the business to his son, and it looks like the young man is keen to make his mark with some new services. Just before reaching the market, you cycle past the architectural practice owned by your old school friend Marie. In her window you notice an advert for 'office layout optimization'.

You head for the library, seeking a book in their reference section. Securing your bike to the cycle rack outside, you walk up the granite steps and through the old oak doors, turning left past the reception desk. You find the book easily enough and sit at one of the large study desks. Turning to the first chapter you begin to read,

Imagine you live in the small, historic market town of Seonsville in southwest France (population five and a half thousand). The population is proud of the old historic market that dominates the town centre.

1.

The Mind Trick That Stops SEO Being Confusing

"Search Engine Optimization" must be one of the most unhelpful labels ever created.

Let me take you back to your recent bike ride into town. You passed signs advertising these services:

- Car engine tuning

- Hybrid power train optimization

- Office layout optimization

It's intuitively obvious what these services do. The first does exactly what it says, with no reordering of words needed: the service provides car engine tuning. The message could not be clearer. The second and third services provide some form of optimization, one with regard to hybrid cars, the other addressing office layout. Even if you're unfamiliar with the technical content of the services themselves, it's clear what each service is offering.

An advertising copywriter might say that the language itself is, "well optimized".

Now apply the same logic to search engine optimization and see how far you get. I'm guessing, not very far. Following the above logic, search engine optimization should be about optimizing search engines. But it's not.

The concepts underpinning Search Engine Optimization are all about optimizing *your website*.

Put like that, it sounds like a great idea. You'd imagine that all business owners would want an optimized website representing their business.

And yet...

I've analysed thousands of websites annually, as part of the Worldwide Digital Footprint Survey. I launched the survey in 2017 and the results clearly show that many businesses are far away from any form of optimized online presence. Leads aren't being generated and sales opportunities are withering on the vine. Money is being left on the table.

Surely no one would spend all that time and effort creating an essential business asset, and then do it in a suboptimal way? But they do. Why does this happen?

The majority of websites are inadequate in how they *attract*, *engage*, and *create a relationship* with the company's perfect clients. A well-optimized website would do this, so it would seem to make sense to have one. In the same way that you'd have a well-tuned car engine or a well-optimized office layout: it's just the commonsense thing to do. Who doesn't want more miles to the gallon (or litres to the kilometre), or an efficient work space?

I believe the very name SEO puts people off. Business owners see it as a distinct and separate thing from their website, and not as an integral part of running an efficient business.

Join me on the journey of rehabilitating SEO, so that it becomes part of the commonsense approach to running a business website in the third decade of the 21st century.

This book will help you optimize your website—its existing content and content you've not yet written.

Time to get cracking.

If you'd like to know when *Lazy Websites Fixed in Five* is published, send an email to:

nextbook@activepresence.com

Further Reading

There are many books to help you improve your website, your business performance, and your personal performance. Here are my favourites (listed alphabetically by the author's surname).

Making Your Website Work: 100 Copy & Design Tweaks for Smart Business Owners
by Gill Andrews

Obviously Awesome: How to Nail Product Positioning so Customers Get It, Buy It, Love It
by April Dunford

The Mom Test: How to talk to customers and learn if your business is a good idea when everyone is lying to you
by Rob Fitzpatrick

The Checklist Manifesto: How to get things right
by Atul Gawande

Zero to Sold: How to Start, Run, and Sell a Bootstrapped Business
by Arvid Kahl

Several Short Sentences About Writing
by Verlyn Klinkenborg

Copywriting Strategies: A No-Nonsense Guide to Writing Persuasive Copy for Your Business
by Nicki Krawczyk

The Subtle Art of Not Giving a F*ck: A Counterintuitive Approach to Living a Good Life
by Mark Manson

Essentialism: The Disciplined Pursuit of Less
by Greg McKeown

Building a Brand Story: Clarify Your Message So Customers Will Listen
by Donald Miller

Deep Work: Rules for Focused Success in a Distracted World
by Cal Newport

Badass: Making Users Awesome
by Kathy Sierra

Built to Sell: Creating a Business That Can Thrive Without You
by John Warrilow

Printed in Great Britain
by Amazon